DISCOVERING YOURSELF

The Key to Understanding Others

DISCOVERING

YOURSELF

The Key to Understanding Others

BOB RIGDON

Tyndale House
Publishers, Inc.
Wheaton, Illinois

Many of the general ideas of this
book were expressed in four
articles written by the author
in the *Tennessee Public Welfare
Record*, 37: *1, 2, 3,* and *4,* 1974.
The author expresses his
gratitude for permission to
quote and develop the principles
in this book.

The material in Chapter 8 first
appeared in the *Tennessee
Public Welfare Record*, 37: *4,*
1974. Used by permission.

First printing, October 1982
Library of Congress Catalog Card Number 82-60250
ISBN 0-8423-0617-X, paper

Printed in the United States of America

With deep gratitude
to my parents
Robert W. (now deceased)
and Dorothy Rigdon
of Topeka, Kansas.
And to my wife, Evelyn,
for the years of help and love.

CONTENTS

A C K N O W L E D G M E N T S

Grateful acknowledgment is given to the following for permission to quote from their materials:

Holt, Rinehart, & Winston, Inc., from the book, *Fundamentals of Human Sexuality* by Herant A. Katchadourian and Donald T. Lunde, ©1972.

Methane, Bob D., from his material presented on Radio Station WSJS, Winston-Salem, N.C.

Oxford University Press, from the book by Ivan Pavlov, *Conditioned Reflexes*, by permission of Oxford University Press.

Restoration Quarterly for material written by the author and published in 1977 and 1978. "The Need of Self Respect and How It Differs from Pride or Conceit," 20:1, ©1977. "The Differentiation of the Need for Sex, Temptation, and Lust," 21:4, ©1978.

Scientific American, S. Coopersmith, "Studies in Self Esteem," February, ©1968.

Tennessee Public Welfare Record, for material written by the author and published in Vol. 37:1, 2, 3, and 4, 1974.

Williams and Wilkins Co., chapter "Sex Hormones and Other Variables in Human Eroticism," by J. Morrey in the book *Sex and Internal Secretions* (Two Volumes), Baltimore, Md., ©1961.

Trainer, Joseph, from the book *Physiologic Foundations for Marriage Counseling*. St. Louis, Mo.: C. V. Mosby Co., ©1965.

Vaillant, George, from the book, *Adaptation to Life*. Boston: Little & Brown & Co., ©1977.

Williams, Eulalie, from the book, *The Spirit and the Forms of Love*, by D.D. Williams, New York: Harper & Row Publishers, ©1968.

I wish to express my thanks to Cecil W. Mann, formerly Head of the Departments of Psychology, Tulane University and Western Carolina University, who taught me some of the main principles developed in this book.

One

The Concept of Order

Among the many factors in human behavior to be understood in order to live more meaningful lives, we would have to include:

> the concept of order
> fear-anxiety
> the needs of humans
> mental health—mental illness
> homeostasis (balance)
> verbal and nonverbal communication
> conscience—self-approval or self-
>   condemnation; guilt

First let's look at the concept of order. This principle is synonymous with, but includes more than, all of the following: structure, congruency, consistency, harmony, cause-effect, what-follows-what, relationships, etc. "What-follows-what" is different from "cause-effect." For instance, I enjoy driving the back roads of the Appalachian Mountains where I live. As I approach every curve, every crest, I am curious to see what is over the ridge, what is beyond the curve. Where I am as I experience that wonderful feeling of anticipation does not *cause* what is over the hill. There is no cause-effect; yet what-follows-what is important in my life and yours.

While driving through Winston-Salem several years ago, I heard the following on radio station WSJS, Winston-Salem, North Carolina, delivered by Bob D. McHone:

> Have you ever noticed ... that what makes life exciting ... is the mystery in it? It's like a bend in the road that beckons us on, or a pathway through the woods. Anything, or any one, we know too well, is less appealing than when something remains hidden ... some element of anticipation, the expectancy of what may be behind the door. That's why we wrap packages. That's why parents hide the Christmas presents from the children ... and also why the children go to bed excited ... and wake up wild with wonder. Imagine, if you can, an elegant dinner ... the table set with fine china, sparkling crystal, and heavy silver. A magnificent tureen of lobster ... and someone lovely to share it with ... and the whole thing lit with powerful floodlights. Too much light does not enable us to see better ... it blinds us. Candlelight is better. A soft light, with the edges undefined, a light that leaves in shadow anything that might distract, and leaves in darkness all the unessentials of the moment. Brilliant light is harsh, repelling. Candlelight is warm and brings us together. The principle applies to other areas. We

should not try to know someone too well, but just accept whatever is revealed by candlelight. We should not try to know everything that lies ahead, around the bend in the road. Life without the mystery would hardly be worth living. It would be like life in the cell of a prison without hope of pardon. We *need* the candlelight, the lure of not quite knowing. The excitement of softness. The river at noon in the glaring sun is not the same as that same river flowing through the twilight when the sun is down behind the valance of the earth.

If you have been absent from your house for a few hours, and, upon your return, one of the hundreds of objects is out of *place* (order), your attention will be drawn to it irresistibly. You will seek a reasonable *explanation* (order) of how, why, and by whom it was moved. If you are unable to find an acceptable *answer* (order), you will be troubled.

You are handed an examination in a college classroom. You hurriedly look it over. Are these the questions you *expected* (order)? Do you know the *answers* (order)? Do you have time to answer all of them? What are your feelings concerning each order? Fearful? Unfair? Sure of yourself? It all depends upon the order's being known or unknown.

You sit down for the first time to drive your new car. How do you *start* it (order)? What is the feel of the steering, gearshift, brakes, etc.? As the days go by, you become accustomed to these different orders. Gradually, you feel more comfortable as the order becomes more known.

Do you remember your first date? How did that feeling compare with your fortieth date with the same person? Did you get to *know* (order) each other?

Think in the same way about your first day at school, at college, at camp, at work.

What about the last book you read? Was it too *simple* (order was grasped too easily)? Did it make *sense* (was there an order to it)?

Why is it that occasionally you meet an individual and very shortly thereafter you feel as though you have known him or her for a long time? Perhaps there was order, personality, attitude, verbal, or nonverbal communication similar to yours or to others with whom you enjoyed a good relationship.

Is not the concept of a belief in order the basis of prediction—whether it is the weather or a mate's behavior? Certainly, there are degrees of accuracy, but the basis of past orders is the principle upon which our suppositions are founded.

Why are some people more intelligent than others, regardless of how you define and measure intelligence? Are they not able to consistently and accurately make finer *discriminations* (order) of words or numbers than others?

What about the creative individuals? They are able to *relate* (order) things in a new or different way. Isn't it disgusting to be playing with word analogies and be unable to find the *common basis* (order)? And then suddenly another person barely glances at it and says, "Oh, these are all verbs, aren't they?"

Why do you and I trust some people? Again, is it not based upon past accumulation of behaviors that did not threaten us? Think about the opposite and the resulting distrust.

Science tries to find the order of things we can measure, the cause-effect, the relationship of all the variables.

Religion tries to answer the question of the order of meaning, purpose, ultimate causes-effects, of things we cannot measure.

Consider the concept of order and our national pastime of sports.

There is extensive "security" offered to the man of sport because the sport scene is one of order, even if it is not idealized. Man learns what the rules of the game are. During the contest the rules remain fixed and decisions become a matter of "living up" to the known. Man comes to sport from a fickle society of changing mores and fluid traditions. Now, present in sport, he faces a cosmos of regulation. The security he lost in "real life" is quickly regained in a stable world of sport. Not only does he know for "sure" what is expected of him, but now he has a group of officials, umpires, commissioners, and the like to make certain he remains within the rules. Deviation is permitted, but one soon learns just how far one can stretch the rules (Slusher, 1967).

Perhaps the basic problem with America is that too many orders are being changed too fast for humans to accept. Toffler's book, *Future Shock,* deals with this basic need of order in life for humans. Stress is caused by a break in order of some type beyond the threshold point of the individual(s).

Why did we have a greater loss of life (percentage-wise) from "natural" deaths among our Korean prisoners of war than in any other known war? They received less physical torture and better food, but the American prisoners died in greater numbers. The Koreans had been trained very effectively to continually break the order of the human need for "love-belongingness" and "self-respect." Stress (broken and unknown orders) takes its toll emotionally and physically. Notice the many research studies on psycho-physiological illnesses that are being published.

When under stress to the point of confusion

or disorientation, many of us resort to numbering consecutively things we never numbered before—objects, ideas, events. "Did I do that first, or did she say that first?" We are trying to restore order to the disorder in our minds. Surely, counting is an absolute order that can be trusted (counted on!). It never varies at all. If only we can find—remember—the sequence, we can solve it! Order is so basic to us.

John N. Bleibtreu writes in *The Parable of the Beast:*

> This new mythology which is being derived from the most painstaking research into other animals, their sensations and behavior, is an attempt to re-establish our losses—to place ourselves anew within an order of things, because faith in an order is a requirement of life.

In the spring of 1924, Ivan Pavlov delivered a lecture reporting the first case of experimental neurosis in a dog. This illustrates the importance of being able to differentiate orders and appropriate responses to separate orders that are similar, yet different. One of his students, Dr. Shenger-Krestovnikova, had conditioned a dog to secrete saliva at the sight of a circle but not at the sight of an ellipse. Then she began to make the ellipse more circular in shape and to present it to the dog. When the ellipse was made almost a perfect circle (ratio of the axis was 8:9) and was presented to the dog, Pavlov said:

> The hitherto quiet dog began to squeal in its stand, kept wriggling about, tore off with its teeth the apparatus for mechanical stimulation of the skin, and bit through the tubes connecting the animal's room with the observer, a behavior which never happened before. On being taken into the experimental room the

dog now barked violently, which was also contrary to its usual custom; in short it presented all the symptoms of a condition of acute neurosis. On testing the cruder differentiations they also were found to be destroyed (Pavlov, 1960).

He commented on another dog's behavior in a similar experiment by Dr. Petrova:

> ... the animal began to enter into a state of general excitation, and ... became quite crazy, unceasingly and violently moving all parts of its body, howling, barking and squealing intolerably. All this was accompanied by an unceasing flow of saliva ... obviously ... this was too difficult a problem for the excitable nervous system of this dog (Pavlov, 1960).

With some dogs, however, the opposite behavior was noticed under similar experiments. These dogs he labeled "inhibitable dogs." Notice Pavlov's descriptions of what occurred:

> ... its secretory effect began to diminish ... practically disappeared ... the animal started this time to lose weight and became very dull (Pavlov, 1960).

Apply and compare this to a child who never knows the order of the behavior of the significant adults in his life. The child says something one day in the presence of his parents, and they laugh. A few days later he repeats it, and this time he is punished. The child is confused; there is no order. He is unable to fathom the situation. If this type of contradictory order is practiced in many aspects of the child's life, involves many different social relationships, and continues over a long period of time, it is very likely that the child's typical behavior could be described by Pavlov's description of the dogs. The child may fight or withdraw. If the behavior becomes more extreme, we label it "manic" or "depressive." Order, and unknown or broken orders, especially in human relationships, serve as a basis for understanding mental health and mental illness. Mental health is a matter of degree, and the degree varies from individual to individual. A broken or unknown order to one person is a challenge; to another it may mean mental illness, acts of hostility, or some other generally undesirable behavior.

If, on the other hand, the order never varies, we label the human feeling that results as "boredom." When bored, humans will break the order. Infants, children, teenagers, husbands, wives, employers, employees, teachers, students—all engage in this reaction to differing degrees. In my own marriage I find myself saying or doing something that irritates my wife. Afterward, I could kick myself. When I can think about it objectively, I realize I did it because I was bored. This concept becomes the basic underlying foundation of discipline problems. When evidence of boredom emerges, the alert teacher breaks the order or offers a new or unknown order. If boredom becomes too great, the student will, out of desperation, break the order himself and likely become a discipline problem.

Is not the principle of gossip many times the filling in of a gap in the order of events—especially "juicy-exciting-forbidden" gaps? Of course, the person who told you can retort, "I didn't say that exactly."

What are jokes? Are they not the totally unexpected, non-threatening breaks in order, or different orders in many cases?

Let us turn to existentialism. Why is there no accepted definition? Because it denies the concept of all I have written. There is no underlying principle of order, but we are told you have to accept that and find meaning in spite of the lack of order. Yet meaning is built on a concept of order. No wonder it is a confusing thought. Some, in trying to be *logical* (follow an order), go one step further: You have to accept that there is no meaning. This leads to the depth of despair and depression.

As individuals, we differ as to the degree of order we need or the degree of the *lack of order* we can tolerate. This is the best way to approach and define stress and coping. The most unknown order we have to deal with eventually is our death. What is that order? The concept of one's going through that order and being raised again is appealing. I want to know that order.

No matter what your philosophical, religious approach to life, there are many questions and problems for which you can find no order, no answer. I solve this by using what I call "suspended judgment." Perhaps someday I will be able to find the order. I will not let it "throw me" mentally or emotionally. That is the best philosophical, religious approach, knowing that "dead-end" questions can always be asked if you—or someone else—is smart enough.

Two

Fear-Anxiety

Why do all humans experience to differing degrees this complex emotion? Generally in psychology we discern the difference between "fear" and "anxiety" as fear being applied to the *specific* and anxiety being applied to the *general* "free-floating" feeling. For the purposes of this book, the two will be combined into the fear-anxiety emotion because I believe that basically, especially on the physiological level, they are the same.

What causes fear-anxiety? Either one of two things. Either the order you are experiencing is unknown, or the order you have known is suddenly broken. Both may even be occurring simultaneously. Consider the example of a girl who begins menstruation without any previous explanation having been given to her. As she becomes aware of the bleeding, she becomes fearful-anxious. This is unknown. "What is happening to me?" She wonders. In her mind, bleeding is always a sign of something serious, a warning. If someone explains the order in an understanding, rational way, this decreases the degree of fear-anxiety. There will probably be some degree of uneasiness, because becoming accustomed to an unknown order by experiencing it over and over is more real than being told about it in symbolic words. It follows, then, that the more we can know about the order of anything, the less we will fear it. A combat veteran once challenged me on this point by saying, "I have been in hundreds of battles, but I am still afraid!" My response was, "Yes, because you never knew when and if the next bullet or bomb had your name on it, and that is a great unknown."

This principle of broken and/or unknown orders applies to the universe. Have you ever experienced an eclipse of the sun without being informed about it beforehand? Even if you were told about it, you probably experienced some fear-anxiety, but to a lesser degree. The principle applies to mechanical things. Recall the broken order of a tire "blowing out" or a light bulb exploding. These illustrations are important, but the order we are interested in explaining in this book is the human order within (intra-human) and the order between and among humans (inter-human), especially the feeling-emotional components. The feeling-emotional components cannot be measured precisely; therefore, we cannot be totally scientific because all scientific methods rely on an accurate unit of measurement. I am cognizant of this and freely admit it.

This is one of the main differences between behavioral psychology as a school (also called the second force) and all other schools of psychology and counseling. I certainly cannot go to the extreme of denying the existence of feelings-emotions because I cannot accurately measure them. The face validity is too strong.

At the same time, I do not want to go to the other extreme of "mysticism." There must be a *rational answer* (order) in between these two extremes.

What Fear Is

There must be a stimulus that we can receive (for example, a loud noise) that communicates a broken and unknown order. When this occurs, it is carried to the brain, which in turn sends out chemical-electrical messages to some of the endocrine glands. These glands secrete hormones, which are carried to all parts of the body almost instantaneously, to prepare the body for action. (We jump.) The extra energy (action) is to restore the broken or unknown order. This is an oversimplification, but describes an important process which must be understood. It is a theory of motivation. This is the order of fear-anxiety. Because many people do not understand this order, they become anxious when they experience anxiety, thus complicating the problem even more. They experience the "snowballing" effect. This principle will be returned to later.

How Do Humans React to Fear-Anxiety?

Certainly, there are individual differences in degree of reaction. Knowing full well the danger of oversimplification, I suggest that the following four reactions are available to humans:

1. fight
2. tremble
3. flee
4. solve rationally

There are times when fighting, trembling, or fleeing are rational, but the general rule is that they are irrational. They do not solve the problem; they do not restore an order with which one can live. I remember going up the steps of a mountain home when suddenly a dog, which I had not seen or heard beforehand, bit my leg. In an instant I was twelve feet across the porch. He came after me, but this time I was prepared. When he lunged, I kicked him with my foot, and fortunately for me, I was successful. I kicked him off the porch. In this incidence, fighting was a rational approach. It would have been irrational to run because he would have caught me. It would have been irrational to only tremble. He would have bitten me again. It would have been irrational to say, "I am a professional counselor, do you have a problem? Would you like to talk about it?"

Consider an example of trembling when it is rational. Suppose you are in the woods and you decide to take a nap. You wake up to find several yellow jackets on your head. Fighting is irrational. I would not advise trying to "kick their teeth out." If you resort to any type of fighting, they will sting you, and I understand more people die of certain types of insect stings than of snake bites each year. You cannot reason with yellow jackets either, so that is irrational. If you can, remain as still as possible. There will be some trembling, but they will not sting you and will eventually leave, restoring your normal order.

Fleeing *can* be rational. For example, you are crossing a street when a car comes bearing down on you at a high rate of speed. Run! That is rational. Don't remain still and tremble! Don't fight! Don't try to talk to the driver!

Let us turn to a husband and wife problem with broken or unknown orders, with fear-anxiety between them. Perhaps if you tried hard enough, you could think of an example when each of the first three reactions are rational, but it is obvious that the general rule is that all three (fighting, trembling, fleeing) are irrational because they do not solve the problem and lessen the fear-anxiety. Some people do resort to fighting, even to the extreme of killing each other. Most murders are committed by family members or close friends of the victim.

Many husbands or wives go through hours, days, weeks, even years of horrendous fear-anxiety because they choose to be still, be quiet, not do anything. They tremble. We say they are nervous wrecks. Some, like Pavlov's "inhibitable" dogs, withdraw into a fantasy world. Yes, they even quit eating or working or having contact with any other human. They begin having hallucinations or delusions. We label them catatonic if their withdrawal-fleeing is too extreme. More people use the withdrawal-trembling approach than the fighting approach. Remember there are degrees of each approach.

Think about the fleeing approach that husbands or wives use. "I'll not go home; I'll find other things to do." "I'll get an additional job—we need the money." We do "rationalize" our irrationality. Some choose not to talk as a way of fleeing. Never ask how her day went, or if you do ask, ask it grudgingly or halfheartedly or cynically so she won't answer. Then you can rationalize that irrationality by saying, "Well, I tried to talk, but she won't respond!" Some ask in the right way but never look at the person in a pleasant manner. Their not looking or looking in an unpleasant way is sure to kill the communication. Then we rationalize that irrationality. We must learn the order of nonverbal communication to live happy lives. This principle will be elaborated upon in Chapter 6.

Murder was suggested as an extreme of fighting. It may be that epilepsy (functional rather than organic epilepsy) is the extreme end result of the internalizing and overuse of trembling as *the* means to deal with broken or unknown orders. Suicide is probably the extreme degree of fleeing.

For nine months the fetus in the mother's

womb becomes accustomed to the order(s) of the sounds of the mother's body, the tactile-touch stimulation of the parts of the womb, constant support, constant temperature, etc. The baby is born, and many orders are changed. At the time of birth, we do have some control over the degrees of change *if* we understand the principle. We know babies give a "startle" response to loud noises, sudden bright lights, being dropped, etc. Each broken order or unknown order brings about chemical-electrical discharges in the baby's body and brain. What if there are too many changes, or the change is too great for the infant over too long a period of time?

Perhaps this is a possible explanation of "Sudden Infant Syndrome" deaths (S.I.D.). They are also called "crib deaths" because they occur in the crib, not in the arms of the mother. Being in a crib is a broken order. Notice the broken orders listed by Dr. Page Hudson, Chief Medical Examiner for the State of North Carolina. "Most studies show that crib deaths hit a peak during the months of December, January, and February." Coldness is a broken order. Hudson reports, "In all cases in which information was available, the infants were bottle fed." The bottle, especially when the infant is not being held, is a broken order of warmth, tactile stimulation, etc. Again, "We have found some evidence of abnormalities in the pancreas of these infants" (Hudson, 1971).

Being overstimulated by too many broken or unknown orders would certainly affect the pancreas, as well as other organs. Of course, we must avoid extremism and simplistic answers. Perhaps there is some truth in F. Leboyer's book, *Birth without Violence,* 1974. There has to be some logical answer to our national problem of a higher infant death rate than many other countries which do not have the skilled physicians and germ-free hospitals that we have.

Many researchers have discovered facts that support the view of the mind-body being inseparable. It might help to think that the connectors between the mind and body are the endocrine glands. I can make myself have a bodily reaction of fear-anxiety by dwelling on some broken order or unknown order between me and another human. If it is severe enough, we call it psychosomatic illness. The newer term is "psychophysiological." It is easily misunderstood. A person may have a malfunctioning organ such as a thyroid gland. The problem may be one of fear-anxiety that has caused the thyroid gland to be overworked to the point that it is enlarged. The cause is emotional, but the problem is a *real* physical problem. It would follow that if the organ damage has not yet reached the point of being irreversible, physical and emotional improvement will result if the person restores order and balance and removes the fear-anxiety. Is this not a logical explanation of people being healed by witch doctors, medicine men, or fortune tellers—anyone they believe in and trust? Most physicians I know tell me at least 50 percent of all patients they treat have problems from these causes (functional in nature) rather than from germs, etc. (organic in nature).

Hans Selye's research is significant in this field. He has written, among numerous publications, *Stress of Life* (1956). J. D. Ratcliff wrote this about Selye's research on rats subjected to broken orders for too long a period of time. "But, suppose the challenge is continuous? Isn't it possible for glands to be worked to death, to be thrown out of chemical kilter . . .? When they [rats] were autopsied the extent of internal wreckage was truly amazing. Adrenals were bloated to three times normal size. There was lymphatic wreckage, ulcers" (Ratcliff, 1963).

Last year several newspapers carried the story from the *Chicago Tribune* reporting Dr. Marilyn Colelin's presentation to the annual meeting of the International Academy of Pathology, United States-Canadian Division meeting, in New Orleans. She reported evidence of fifteen people "frightened to death. . . . The heart cells were killed by the body's reaction to fear" ("Doctor Will Offer First Evidence," February 24, 1980).

Drs. Joel Dimsdale and Jonathan Moss reported on a recent development that makes possible a more exact and on-going measurement of epinephrine (adrenaline) and norepinephrine. This is a major breakthrough to help us better understand hormones. The conclusion of their specific research is:

> Under circumstances of intense physical activity or anxiety, the body is exposed to concentrations of norepinephrine that are three times higher, or epinephrine two times higher, than what is experienced during alert, active conversation. Such sizeable increases in catecholamine levels may provide some insight into the often quoted relationship between emotional arousal and cardiac pathology . . . (Dimsdale and Moss, 1980).

Earlier, I suggested as the cause of the high incidence of deaths among the American prisoners of war in the Korean conflict this same concept applied to broken or unknown orders of love-belongingness and self-esteem.

Dr. W. E. Mayor, psychiatrist, reported on Korean "brainwashing" on November 27, 1956. Summarizing the salient points of brainwashing, he notes:

> Something goes on between and among people . . . to interfere with normal relationships. Indoctrination begins with a Korean speaking fluent English, not dressed in a military uniform, and extremely friendly, explaining he

did not want to be there any more than the Americans did. "So, why don't we cooperate, and then there will be no exquisite oriental torture. Don't try to escape, listen to us and think. You don't have to accept what we say." Next, they isolated the leaders and different races. To accomplish their goals, the Koreans corrupted the communication. No snapshots or "good news" letters were delivered. Divorce notices, "Dear John" letters, and collection threats were all delivered without delay. Informing on each other was encouraged and rewarded. After an accumulation of these broken orders were built up, the G.I.'s quit trusting each other. They backed off emotionally from each other. Not one American escaped. Four out of ten died, which is an extremely high death rate under the physical circumstances. Of those that survived, only one of five accepted a free call home. They did not get over these attitudes very quickly. A three year follow up indicated a high degree of emotional withdrawal behavior among the survivors.

When one contrasts boredom (the order known too well for too long a period of time) which can result in an undersupply of hormones to energize us and fear-anxiety which can result in an oversupply of hormones, stimulating us too much, one begins to understand the extremely broad range of human feelings and actions. It is very helpful even if it is oversimplified. Logically, one can understand what physicians mean when they say to a family, "If he doesn't find a meaning or purpose or reason for living, he will die." The proper amount of flow of hormones is necessary to happiness and well-being. We express it as, "We like a challenge!" Notice the following continuum line:

Figure 1
Degrees of a Break in Order of an Unknown Order:

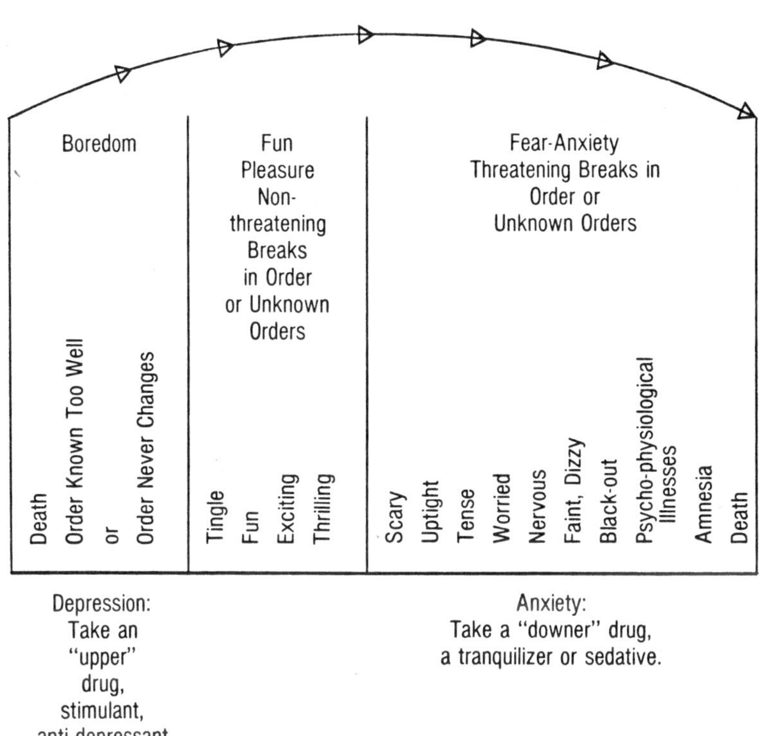

Remember, our endocrine glands can be stimulated to secrete hormones by thought processes alone, as well as external stimuli of events, humans, and objects.

We all want to be in the nonthreatening range of Figure 1. Effective living is learning how to handle the stress to the left or to the right without going too far to the other extreme. A "bored" teenager who drives 120 miles per hour for "kicks" or a person who suffers from a divorce and withdraws socially and professionally is an example of this type of extremism.

"Drugs," generally speaking, are divided into

two categories—"uppers" and "downers"—as any high school student will tell you. Why do people take drugs? They take them to be happy. If you are too uptight, take a downer. If you are bored and want excitement, take an upper. But there are serious drawbacks to chemical solutions. Again oversimplifying, the results are often psychological addiction to uppers and physical addiction to downers. Psychological addiction means dependence on a chemical for fun, happiness, etc., rather than learning how to live effectively. Physiological addiction means the body requires increasingly more of the chemical to produce the desired effect. In addition, delirium tremens usually occur upon withdrawal. Any drug taken to excess is dangerous. Deciding you will never take a drug, even under a physician's prescription, is a foolish extreme. However, the goal should be effective living without chemical props insofar as is possible.

T. H. Homes and R. H. Rahe have devised what they call "The Social Readjustment Rating Scale." From their research, they assigned point values which ranged from 100-0 to "Life Events." Some are as follows: Death of spouse—100 (the highest stressful life event); Personal injury or illness—53; Marriage—50; Sex difficulties—39; Trouble with in-laws—29; Change in eating habits—15, etc. They also found that happy events (such as marriage) can create some stress. The accumulation of stressful events over a short period of time seems to be the most important finding. They report that 80 percent of the individuals whose total point value reached 300 over a two-year period of time became physically ill, whereas only 33 percent of the individuals whose point value reached 150—199 became ill.

Hopefully, this chapter enables us to better understand the emotion(s) of fear-anxiety. It is built upon the basis of "order" being the great foundation principle of understanding humans. Broken or unknown orders create in our minds and bodies that which we label fear or anxiety. We are motivated by the flow of hormones to restore the order, to find the order of the unknown, or to place ourselves within a new order that is understandable. The extremes of boredom or anxiety are poles on a continuum line far apart but connected by this concept. A general rule is that it is the accumulation of many small "happenings" that creates happiness or misery. Seeking the one big event in life is not the answer to effective living.

Three

Needs of Humans

What do we mean by needs? What is it that humans need? Some restrict the word "need" to only those things necessary for physical life. In this book we will discuss those needs, in addition to others that add meaning, purpose, well-being, and contentment to life. As stated before, it is most difficult to measure these concepts because of the lack of a precise or dependable unit of measurement; but these things are what most of us are truly, eagerly seeking to aid our everyday, minute-by-minute living.

Many people have written on the subject of needs: H. A. Murray in the 1930s, A. H. Maslow in the 1950s, John C. Flannagan in 1978, George Vaillant in 1980, and Angus Campbell in 1980, to name a few. I would suggest the following list of needs as a beginning point.

1. physical
2. safety-security
3. love-belongingness (nonsexual)
4. self-esteem-respect
5. play-laughter-humor
6. information
7. understanding-wisdom
8. beauty-aesthetic
9. self-actualization
   a. to become all one is capable of becoming
   b. religious
      (1) Where did I come from?
      (2) Why am I here?
      (3) Where am I going? (Maslow, 1970, adapted)

There are a few individuals who are exceptions in that they seem to possess happiness in spite of the absence of one or more of these needs. However, the vast majority of us seem to experience all of these needs, never all at once, but all at different times and to different degrees. The exceptions do not destroy the concept.

The needs that arise within us are the basic foundation to explain intra-order in humans. An unfamiliar need that arises, or a need that is unfulfilled but concerning which we do not understand the proper order to fulfill, creates some degree of fear-anxiety. Pain, discomfort, sadness, etc., are signals that something is wrong with need-fulfillment. We are motivated to avoid pain, discomfort, and sadness. The emotion we label "hate" quite often arises when we perceive someone interfering with our need fulfillment as we perceive it. Jealousy is the emotion that surfaces when we are afraid someone will take away some element(s) or person(s) we perceive as necessary to our need fulfillment. Envy is the emotion experienced when we fail in need fulfillment and observe someone else who is successful in the same need fulfillment that we lack.

Maslow (1970) suggested a hierarchical order of prepotency that is useful in varying degrees to explain more order or lack of it in need fulfillment. If we become hungry enough, we are not interested in any of the other needs from level two through nine. No doubt, physical needs are the most basic. Again, do not find an exception and think the exception destroys the general rule for humans. If we are fearful (level two unfulfilled) to too great a degree, the needs from level three to level nine are nonexistent. We know they are there, but they are latent—nonmotivating. The hierarchical order is inexact and varies, but it does exist and is most useful in explaining or giving an order to otherwise confusing and seemingly contradictory human behaviors.

Another useful concept is to realize that probably all of our needs are circular in nature. If you can, imagine a dot moving around a circle (Figure 2). Where the dot is in Figure 2 might represent three hours after eating. Your body is "using up" the food you ingested. In a few more hours, the dot will be at the point marked unfulfilled; you are hungry. If it stays there for more than a few days, you will become starved. If it continues there, deprivation may result in death. When the dot reaches "unfulfilled," you will be motivated to seek food. Under normal circumstances, you will eat; and while you are eating, the dot moves toward "fulfilled." If you eat enough food, the dot will be at "fulfilled." As soon as you stop, it will begin moving again.

It is obvious that this continues throughout life. When a need is fulfilled, we label it pleasure. Unfortunately, most of us use the word "love" when it would be better to call it "pleasure." Notice how we say, "I just love seafood; I love a good joke; I love good music," and so on. (In the following chapter, love will be discussed in detail, but these examples reveal some

Figure 2
The Circular Nature of Human Needs
The passage of time will move a need from fulfillment
to unfulfillment—nothing has to happen!

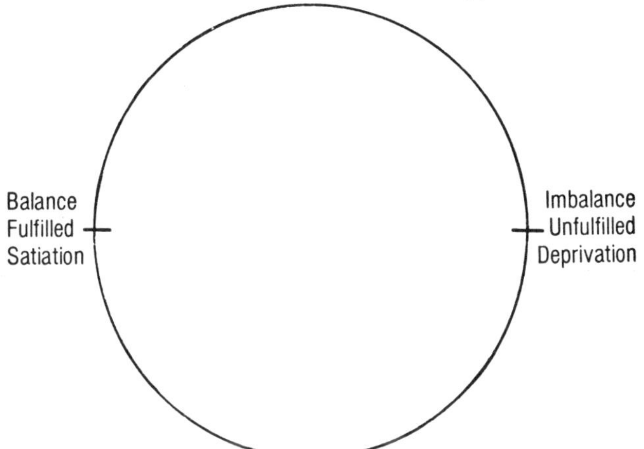

Some needs are fulfilled by input: Hunger—Food
Some needs are fulfilled by output: Activity—Work

of our great confusion about the subject.)

In returning to the point of eating until your need of food is fulfilled, sometimes you continue to eat. What occurs then? Any need that has been satisfied and is fulfilled again before the dot has time to move to unfulfillment brings satiation and results in: (1) the act of fulfillment losing its pleasure, followed by (2) a "pushing away" or withdrawal behavior, and (3) hostile-fighting behavior if satiation continues.

Think about your experiences at family reunions. You eat all that good food, and it is extremely pleasurable. You are full. Then your favorite aunt approaches you saying, "You are not going to hurt my feelings, are you? Have a piece of my chocolate cake." You don't want it, but you eat it anyway. It may actually be painful. However, as I am writing this, it is 10 A.M. and I had only a piece of toasted bread for breakfast. If the same aunt handed me a piece of the same cake right now, I would be delighted. What is the difference? In the language of the dot on the circle, the dot is at the point of my need for hunger being unfulfilled. When I was at the family reunion, it would have been ridiculous to blame my lack of pleasure, even pain, on my aunt, the cake, or myself.

Apply the same reasoning to all needs and all human relationships. Specifically, in sexual need fulfillment we err many times by not understanding the circular principle. We blame our husband, or wife, or the technique, or the act itself; or we blame ourselves for the lack of pleasure in sexual intercourse when many times we are trying to fulfill a need that is already satiated. What would you think if I, when satiated with food and after forcing my aunt's chocolate cake down, had said to her, "I'm going to find an aunt who really knows *how* to bake chocolate cake!" Of course, it is unfair. But we do the same to each other many times because of our ignorance of the order of intra-human needs.

We now know that the average time of the dot moving on the circle of sexual need fulfillment is quite different for male and female at the physical level only. The average adult male accustomed to sexual intercourse needs fulfillment once every three days, while the average adult female accustomed to sexual intercourse needs sex approximately once every thirteen days (Money, 1961; Trainer, 1965). Thankfully, this difference can be surmounted by understanding and applying the other types of love which will be discussed in Chapter 4.

The principle of the dot moving from fulfillment to unfulfillment is useful in understanding *every* need, and properly applied, leads to happier individuals. Another vital thought at this point is that *nothing has to happen* for the dot to move from fulfillment to unfulfillment. We use the need fulfillment up; it becomes depleted.

When I first began counseling, I was always looking for what happened to cause the problem. Now I feel more successful because I also look for what ceased happening that at one time was refilling a depleted need. Over the years I have discovered it is the accumulation of many small events that is the key to enduring happiness or to nagging misery. Most humans do not understand this concept and are looking for something big or sensational to bring them happiness.

Quite often in a counseling situation a wife will explain to me why she is sure her husband no longer loves her. She is having a difficult time putting it into words and often it will come out something like this: "Let me give you an example. If the toilet paper runs out, he will not put a new roll in the holder. He will leave it on the floor for weeks. I have to put it in the holder." Others will express similar consternation about his dirty clothes, burned-out light bulbs, or broken screen doors.

Now all of these negligent acts by themselves are small, insignificant events, but they have accumulated over time, perhaps qualitatively as well, until she, in adding them together, concludes he doesn't care (love) about her as he formerly did. He once was more thoughtful. When men realize their wives are unhappy, they may resort to buying them expensive gifts, mistakenly thinking that will make everything agreeable again. If the same behavior concerning small things continues or steadily increases, the problem continues, growing even worse.

Our mind is like an adding machine that keeps a running total of the negative, small events that keep *each* need unfilled and also a summation of the positive small events that fulfill each need. It is the sum total, not one big occurrence, that makes the difference in most human relationships. Many trivial incidents outweigh one extravagant event, most of the time. Verbal and nonverbal communication pertaining to all thoughts, speech, and deeds that convey meanings to others will be discussed in Chapters 6 and 7. It is the sum total of the multitude of small things that results in either positive or negative need fulfillment. Life is complicated, but not hopeless. There are answers.

In reflecting over the material discussed in this chapter, it should be obvious that to differing degrees we are *dependent on others* for each need being fulfilled. It is serious to err by going to either extreme on this point. Some go astray by internalizing, "I don't need anyone." Others believe *everyone* must like them; therefore, they go to pieces if one person snubs them. Both extremes are fatal to one's emotional health. Donne stated a truth: "No man is an island."

In lecturing on this point, I formerly said, "Now there are exceptions to this concept of dependence, such as not being dependent on others for the air we breathe." But as we learn more about pollution, including others' cigarette smoking, I cannot use that example anymore. In fact, I am hard pressed to find an exception wherein I am totally independent. Humans do need humans, at least to some degree. Social psychology and sociology are intriguing areas of study. A common characteristic of most assassins is that they are extreme loners—isolates. At the same time, most studies of self-actualized people reveal they require some private time to be totally alone for a while. At birth a human is the most helpless for the longest period of time of all living creatures. How old would a human have to be just to physically survive, let alone emotionally survive? One week? A year? Two years? Four years? Six years? We need at least one other older human. We live in dyads, triads, and groups. It does not hurt my ego to fully, completely say, "I need my wife, my children, my parents, my friends." I feel sympathy for those who think such statements are degrading, and I fear what the future holds for those who sincerely feel that way. Equally, I fear for the future of those who go to the other extreme. Basic internalizations—principles ingrained until we think we were born with them—affect the outcome of our lives.

We are dependent on others, but *we are not helpless.* By my actions I can motivate others to help in fulfilling my needs. As an infant, I am, perhaps, totally helpless, but that does not last long, as any parent can testify. The goal should be to mutually satisfy each other's needs, not only to have personal needs satisfied while ignoring the needs of others. Likewise, we should not embrace the other extreme of internalizing that we should satisfy others, regardless, and never receive any reward here or in the hereafter. Many religious people have falsely internalized the concept that if they are rewarded, their good deed is nullified. Do not misunderstand the goal of mutual satisfaction by thinking that every situation will be reciprocal in nature. You may sincerely help an individual to satisfy his need and receive nothing from him. If, however, you practice this kind of life over a period of time with many individuals, enough of them will respond positively so that your needs will be met. In that sense, it is reciprocal.

To clarify the concept of need fulfillment contrasted with the two extremes, look at Figure 3.

Apply the diagram to any need and its fulfillment or lack of fulfillment. For example, consider self-esteem and one small way it is fulfilled. Suppose you find a necktie that is extremely attractive to you and looks great with a certain suit. You are wearing your tie and a person sincerely, genuinely, without any ulterior motive (as you perceive it), compliments your tie. Being a gracious person, you sincerely, spontaneously thank the person. That is pleasurable to a degree—

Figure 3
Degrees of Need Fulfillment

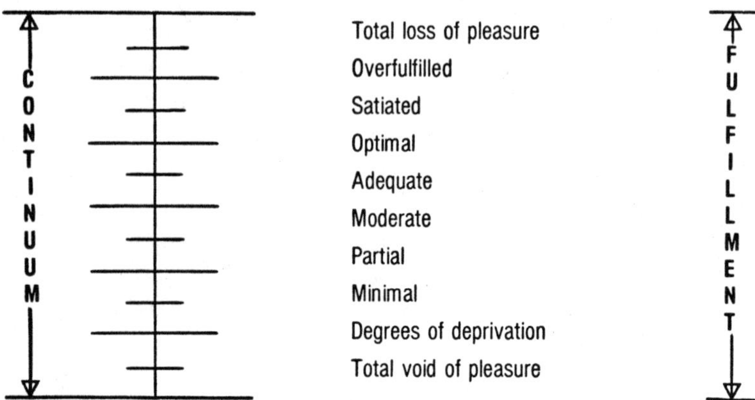

probably adequate or optimal would be the location as it has been depicted in Figure 3. Next, suppose the person begins to leave your presence but stops, turns around, and says some more complimentary things. If this continues, the need of self-esteem will move to "overfulfilled" or "satiated," or even to a total loss of what was once pleasurable. You will probably try to excuse yourself. If that doesn't work, you might become hostile over the situation.

A second example illustrates the other extreme concerning the same necktie. Suppose you wear it on ten different occasions, and no one seems to notice. In fact, you have caught a few looking at it with an expression which you interpret as horror. It does not take many incidents like this before a total void of pleasure concerning your tie permeates your mind at the emotional level, and you begin to question your ability to select neckties. However, if several people compliment it and look at it with admiration without going to extremes, you feel good and your self-esteem is enhanced. This is the essence of Cooley's Looking Glass Theory and Robert Bierstedt's statement: "I am not what I think I am. I am not what you think I am. I am what I think you think I am." An addition to improve it would be: "I am what I think the consensus of others' thinking of me to be."

Now consider Figure 4.

Figure 4
Degrees of Variation in Ways Needs Are Fulfilled

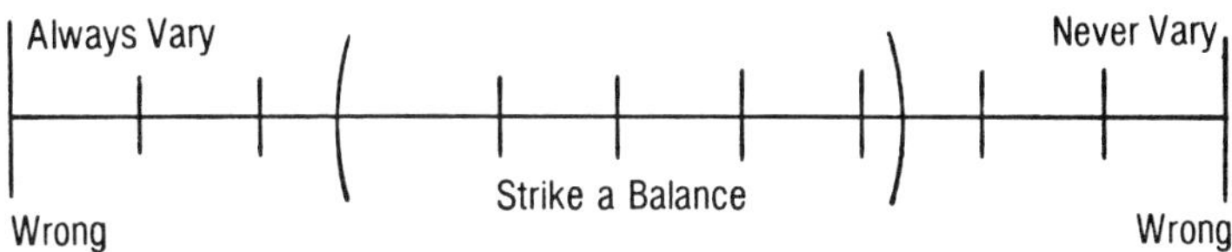

Here again, humans deplete their pleasure by fixating at one extreme or the other. I know a man who never varied as far as anyone could determine in his daily routine of arising, eating the same breakfast, catching the same bus, doing the same work at the same location (which was repetitious work), having the same lunch at the same place, riding the same bus home, and eating the same supper. Every Saturday and Sunday were the same as every other Saturday or Sunday. He never went anywhere for a vacation. He committed suicide. The same order performed in the same way is boredom. Humans cannot tolerate that. On the other hand, I have read of a woman who would never wear the same dress twice. Almost every order in her life was continually varied until she had to be institutionalized because of hallucinations and delusions. Most of us are not that extreme; yet the principle accounts for many hitherto puzzling emotions and actions.

Personally, if all the orders in my life are going smoothly and have for several days, as I sit down to the usual (same order) meal my wife cooks, I may say, "Honey, can't we have something different?" She takes note of that and one week later goes to a lot of trouble and expense to cook a brand new dish. However, during the week many orders of mine have been broken. The boss "jumps on me." I have forgotten two important appointments; two patients are presenting me with a dilemma for which I have no answer; and the car needs repairing. What happens when I arrive home and sit down to that new dish? I probably will say, "Why can't we have the same thing we enjoy so much?" Under her breath, my wife is saying, "Men! Who can understand them? You make me furious!" This is one small example of inconsistent behavior that occurs throughout life, but there is an answer (an order) to this perplexity. By this we understand that you cannot totally isolate any one area or need fulfillment in your life. All overlap and affect each other in varying degrees.

Stress is any need unfulfilled or maladaptively fulfilled. We are much better at verbally describing unfulfilled needs in a specific way than verbalizing a fulfilled need. Look at the list in Figure 4 and the words following the $\neq$ sign (which indicates the common label when this need is unfulfilled). Slang words are even more common.

Specific Labels When a Need Is Unfulfilled
Level I Needs

   Food = hungry, malnutrition, starvation
   Water = thirsty, dehydrated
   Air = can't breathe, suffocating, choking, asphyxiation
   Rest, sleep = tired, worn out, fatigued, exhausted
   Activity, work, play = need to get out and do something
   Body elimination = constipation
   Minerals, vitamins = deficiency

> Sex (eros love) = need a mate
> To bear or father a child = want a baby
> To be physically well = sick, diseased
> To be warm = chilled, cold
> To be cooler = hot

Level II Needs
> Safety-security = afraid, fearful, scared

Level III Needs
> Play-laughter = sad, nothingness, bored

Level IV Needs
> Love-belongingness (nonsexual) = lonely, al-
> ienated, estranged, unloved, hated, friend-
> less, no roots, no family

Level V Needs
> Self-respect, esteem, worth, dignity, regard,
> concept = worthless, useless, not needed,
> blue, blahs, depressed, suicidal

Level VI Needs
> Information = dumb, stupid, ignorant

Level VII Needs
> Understanding, wisdom = educated fool,
> idiot

Level VIII Needs
> Aesthetic, beauty = uncultured

Level IX Needs
> Self-actualization (to become all you are
> capable of becoming) = cheated, unful-
> filled, left out in life
> Religion = lost, unsaved, condemned

Certainly, the words are inexact and overlapping in many instances; yet they convey deep human meaning. There are probably other needs that time and mind will isolate and label, but the foregoing give us a broad framework of the order within us. We use general labels to describe almost any frustrated, unfulfilled, or maladaptively fulfilled need—stress, frustration, anger, anxiety, hurt, hopelessness, confusion, etc. If my reasoning is correct, the bottom line is always a need not being fulfilled in a "right" way.

Common Problems with Need Fulfillment

1. The first problem is so simple it is often overlooked. Many people do not know what needs they have. From counseling experience, I have listened to many human miseries being unfolded to me verbally and nonverbally. It becomes clear in many cases that a person's self-esteem is unfulfilled; yet if I suggest that this is the problem, the reply is often, "What is that?" When we are fortunate enough, by working together, to fulfill this need for the person over a period of time, it is amazing to watch the change. I have found the same lack of knowledge concerning sexual needs. Counselors should never assume any knowledge is common.

2. Second, experiences over the last fifty years, especially the past twenty-seven, reveal that humans have the common problem of denying the reality of their needs. Although a need is clearly there, they repress it and refuse to discuss it. Many fit into this category. How sad that these people have internalized a set of values that are contrary to their human nature. The previous sentence should not be taken to an erroneous extreme, as implying that unrestricted impulse gratification or uncontrolled need fulfillment is being suggested. Certainly individuals, families, communities, or nations cannot exist for very long if a majority of people believe and act in such a manner. Most of the time my needs and your needs can be fulfilled in such a way that others can live effective lives while you are doing the same. Regardless of philosophical, religious, or nonreligious orientation, mutual-reciprocal need

fulfillment has to be a goal for rational people. If we believe in a Creator, we must believe in the Creator's order that makes possible the fulfillment of the needs the Creator placed within us.

3. Third, a common problem with needs is that often we know and do not repress the fact of a need within us, but we do not understand *how* to fulfill that need. In our university, students who confide in me often say with despair, "I am so lonely. How do you make friends?" Perhaps in the United States this is the main problem—*unfulfilled nonsexual love.* This is the reason that much of this book will be devoted to the subject of love.

Unfulfilled self-esteem is probably the second greatest problem in America. Sexual problems would rank third.

4. Fourth, some people's lives are filled with tension and turmoil because they do not know how to fulfill a need without *interfering with others fulfilling their needs.* For example, a person may maladaptively fulfill his or her need of self-esteem by "putting others down," always finding fault in others, looking for mistakes to hold against them. Such people are destroying the other person's self-esteem in order to build up their own. It will not work because we are dependent on others to a great degree to fulfill our own need of self-esteem.

5. Fifth, sometimes we defeat ourselves by fulfilling one of our needs in a manner that *interferes with the fulfillment of another need.* Often I deal with one who is satisfying his need for sexual intercourse in a way that violates his conscience and hence interferes with his self-esteem being fulfilled. He is in opposition to himself. Oversimplifying the total problem-solving approach, it may be stated that you have two choices:

a. Change the way of fulfilling your need so that it harmonizes with your value system.

b. Change your value system so that it harmonizes with the way you are fulfilling your needs.

The "bottom line" of the two statements is to find a congruent order to bring internal peace. All people have values—they are just different values. Many therapists, probably most, choose one of the two above approaches, depending on what the counselor's value system dictates on the given problem. This is an over-simplification but an excellent point for all of us to consider. Dr. O. S. Walters wrote, "Accumulated evidence indicates that no primitive people is without conception of right and duty" (Walters, 1974). Most therapists and all humans impose their values on others at the nonverbal communication level, regardless of intentions. To be honest in a tactful manner is probably wiser than pretending to be valueless or saying, "It makes no difference to me what you do," when your nonverbal communication is telling the person it does make a difference.

6. Sixth, from the fifth difficulty flows another problem which occurs often enough that it must be stated. Some people have a *value system that denies the fulfillment of a need* by any human, in any way, at any time. This has to be a wrong value system. Humans usually experience it at the sexual need level and at the self-esteem need level. For them, the only hope is to change their value system so that in some way both needs can be fulfilled in an acceptable manner.

7. This common problem with need fulfillment may be stated as *not belonging to a reference group that supports us* in our methods of fulfilling our needs. Please look for the reasonableness in the preceding sentence before taking it to extremes at which it becomes void of meaning. People gravitate to people of similar values. Concerning this aspect of our dependency on other humans, Dr. R. D. Allen wrote that the most

effective way to maintain or change human behavior in principle, is social peer pressure (Allen, 1933). Since humans are social in nature, they cannot find happiness in a social vacuum. If we join a formal or informal reference group in which most members fulfill each of their needs in a way that is in general harmony with the way we fulfill our needs, then all goes well emotionally. However, if we become a member of a reference group that fulfills its needs in a way different from our way, emotional incongruence—turmoil—will usually result. Support from other human beings seems to be a necessity for the vast majority of humans. Of course, that does not mean that everyone must approve of our method of fulfilling our needs. Reference groups are simply groups of humans we look to for appropriate ways of thinking, speaking, and behaving to fulfill our needs. There are formal groups such as clubs and churches and informal groups such as the people with whom we eat lunch or attend sports events.

8. Logically, the next common problem interfering with our happiness, our need fulfillment, is *attempting to maintain membership in two reference groups that are diametrically opposed as to how to fulfill one's needs.*

In our town there was a men's club that seemed to have existed for the purpose of getting together on Friday nights, becoming drunk, and staying drunk until Sunday night. The wives of several of the men in this reference group sometimes appeared in my office for marital-family counseling. It is impossible to maintain membership in such a group and in a family at the same time. One year at our university there were eight or nine attempted suicides. All but one could be explained by this problem of contradictory reference groups. The students tried to become members of a reference group at college that used illegal drugs or engaged in some behavior (usually sexual) that was the opposite of the values held by their family reference group.

Alcoholics Anonymous has more success combatting alcoholism than I or any other therapist I know. Why? Social peer pressure is the answer. It is true, however, that if a businessman ("white collar") enters an AA group which is composed mainly of "blue collar" men, he is not as likely to succeed as he would be with his peers; that is, other white collar workers. The words *peer pressure* are vital. Have you ever known an alcoholic to quit drinking and stay sober while continuing to run around with his old cronies who drink? I haven't known such a person.

9. The ninth common problem of need fulfillment refers to the fact that *many humans have been molded by significant others*, mothers, fathers, etc., to either fight, tremble, or flee when they sense an unfulfilled need rather than to fulfill a need in a rational manner. Any one of a combination of irrational reactions found in Figure 5 is possible.

Figure 5

Possible Categories of How Humans
React to Unfulfilled Needs

1. Fight	Thoughts	Speech	Actions	Extreme—Murder
2. Tremble	Thoughts	Speech	Actions	Extreme—Functional Epilepsy
3. Flee	Thoughts	Speech	Actions	Extreme—Suicide
4. Solve Rationally	Thoughts	Speech	Actions	Need Successfully Fulfilled—Happiness

Refer to the chapter on fear-anxiety for more understanding of this concept.

Suppose as a child you were brought up in a home with the pattern of fighting. For instance, your father attempts to move the chair at the breakfast table, but it is stuck to the floor by the wax. In rage, he kicks it. In fact, most of the time any order for him is broken, he reacts by fighting in some manner. Very likely, if you admire your father at all, you will be a "fighter." If you suffer or if your mother (whom you like more than your father) suffers, you may go to one of the other extremes of trembling or fleeing. Extremes beget extremes!

Human reactions to a broken order or unknown order of an automobile reflect clearly the irrationality of fighting, trembling, or fleeing. Suppose you are by yourself driving on a deserted road in the middle of the night, and the red warning light "oil" comes on. How will you react? Some immediately resort to fighting, perhaps just thinking fighting thoughts. Some will fight by words; some will fight by actions, stopping the car, slamming the door, kicking a tire, and raising the hood up with such strength it comes out of alignment. Every once in a while we read of a person taking a gun and shooting a car that he labels a "lemon."

Some of us are tremblers. We become so nervous we run a stop light; our nervousness causes the car to weave. A few have anxiety attacks, cannot focus their eyes, have a headache, etc.

Some people flee. They refuse to look at the illuminated light. They force themselves to think about something else, ignoring the problem completely. I have known a few people who have parked the car and actually abandoned it. If you will apply the same principles to human relations, an understanding of how we react to broken or unknown orders in marriages or families begins to emerge. Concerning the automobile, if you do not know the order of determining the seriousness of the oil light's coming on, the only rational thing to do is to stop and have the car towed to one who does understand, because an automobile engine can be ruined in a few blocks of driving if, indeed, it has no oil pressure.

You may think of a few exceptions, but remember they are exceptions, not rules. The preceding is a rational way of reacting which is not fighting, trembling, or fleeing. One of the purposes of this book is to communicate information so that humans can rationally solve problems within themselves and between and among humans. We must know the order before we can react rationally; otherwise, it is all left to chance, to irrational ways of responding.

To overcome twenty to thirty years of fighting, trembling, or fleeing is not easy, but it can be done by most people. My approach is one of using both insight and practice (behaving), not always just one approach. Most therapists are either "insight" or "action" therapists or combinations of both (London, 1964). For some *few* counselees, only one approach is necessary.

10. The tenth common problem of need fulfillment is that many people believe *oversatiation* —overfulfillment—of a need will bring more happiness. Perhaps this came out of the other extreme of the depression years of the thirties when people were deprived of the most basic physical needs. That suffering left an indelible mark emotionally on so many humans. You have heard them say, "No child of mine will suffer as I did." World War II and the following years of prosperity came, and we couldn't get enough, or so we thought. Our children, however, not having experienced a financial depression, began acting strangely, we thought. Many exploded in the sixties, actually throwing "materialism" into the face of their parents. The parents were bewildered. "Why are you a hippie?

You had clothes, bicycles, cars, stereos. If I had one present for Christmas in the thirties, I would have been overjoyed.'' Anger, total emotional breaks occurred in families. The Vietnam War was only the catalyst, not the cause.

The parents, by lavishing on their children gifts of which they could not even dream, were sure they were "loving" their children, but the children didn't perceive it that way. Why? Because any need fulfilled and then continually overfulfilled loses its pleasure. This pleasure we wrongly made synonymous with love. Do not be mistaken. If a need is unfulfilled for a long period of time, and you fulfill it for me, I interpret that as love, but oversatiation of any need is not love. Also, there is a need of love within and by itself as well as love connected with help in fulfilling an unfulfilled need.

11. The eleventh problem of need fulfillment is the error of *fixating* at one need level and ignoring the other needs within us. There is the story of a man who was almost killed by a terrible house fire as a boy. Afterward, he became obsessed with the need of safety concerning fire to the point that other needs were non-existent in his awareness, but at the unconscious level they were crying out. Frustrated needs, denied needs, insist on expression, and sometimes it is strange indeed how they manifest themselves. Total repression of other needs to fixate at one level of need fulfillment will not yield a happy life.

Last of all, many humans are perplexed as to how to handle an unfulfilled need, when for a period of time it is impossible to fulfill a specific need. Thankfully, the "Grant Study" research has been completed which helps in solving this dilemma. George Vaillant reported the results of this research which involved 268 men over a thirty-five-year period. The book is *Adaptation to Life.* The part which is applicable to our purposes here is labeled in the appendix "Mature Mechanisms."

These mechanisms are common in "healthy" individuals ages twelve to ninety. For the users these mechanisms integrate reality, interpersonal relationships and private feelings. To the beholder they appear as convenient virtues. Under increased stress they may change to less mature mechanisms.

Altruism. Vicarious but constructive and instinctually gratifying service to others. . . . Altruism . . . provides real, not imaginary, benefit to others . . . it leaves the person using the defense at least partly gratified.

Humor. Overt expression of ideas and feelings without individual discomfort or immobilization and without unpleasant effect on others . . . humor lets you call a spade a spade; . . . *humor* permits one to bear and yet to focus upon what is too terrible to be borne. . . .

Suppression. The conscious or semiconscious decision to postpone paying attention to a conscious impulse of conflict . . . includes looking for silver linings, minimizing acknowledged discomfort, employing a stiff upper lip, and deliberately postponing but not avoiding. . . .

Anticipation. Realistic anticipation of or planning for future inner discomfort . . . includes goal directed but [not] overly careful planning or worrying, [not] premature but realistic affective anticipation of death or surgery, separation, and the conscious utilization of "insight." . . .

Sublimation. Indirect or attenuated expression of instincts without either adverse consequences or marked loss of pleasure. It includes both expressing aggression through pleasurable games, sports, and hobbies; and romantic attenuation of instinctual expression during a real courtship . . . instincts are channeled rather than dammed or diverted. Successful artistic expression remains the classic example. . . . In *sublimation*, feelings are acknowledged, modified and directed toward a relatively significant person or goal so that modest instinctual satisfaction results (Vaillant, 1977).

Here are five ways of adapting to and coping with a need we cannot fulfill. First, we should seek a way or ways to fulfill a need in a rational manner. This is the only completely satisfactory answer. Even these mature mechanisms should not be relied upon until all rational avenues of need fulfillment are explored.

Four

Love

Karl Menninger's words are implanted deeply in my thoughts:

> When the scientist begins to talk about love, he is between Scylla and Charybdis. If he adheres rigidly to the conventional language and formulae of science, he will end in that same sterile futility that has long characterized science in its application to human social life. If on the other hand, he abandons his scientific habits for a greater reliance upon intuitive truth, he risks verging upon the sentimental and the poetic. Sentiment and poetry are not necessarily antithetical to truth, but the scientist who uses poetic terms is likely to be as discredited as a poet who uses scientific ones (Menninger, 1942).

Scientists depend upon one of several forms of "scientific method," all of which depend upon a precise unit of measurement, and therein is the center of the problem. What is the unit of measurement of love? As is true with all emotions, we have no unit of measurement. What shall we do then? Deny all emotions as the extreme behaviorists do?

Thorndike wrote in 1918, "Whatever exists at all exists in some amount" (Munn, 1962). Others reasoned: "If it exists, then it can be measured"; and next, "If I can't measure it, it does not exist." The last statement belongs to the "empirical positivism" school of philosophy. I reject the basic reasoning as false. Things, events, emotions can and do exist. The face validity is too strong. Whenever there is a precise unit of measurement, use it in the appropriate scientific method approach, but do not reject those things that do not have a precise unit of measurement. Admit the problem and continue to study the subject. This is what I am doing, especially concerning "love."

Allport, in criticizing Freud and McDougall, wrote:

> A persistent defect of modern psychology is its failure to make a serious study of the affiliative desires and capacities of human beings. If I am not mistaken, only two sustained theories concerning their nature have been developed. Both seem to me somewhat abortive. One is the approach of those writers who postulate a _gregarious_ instinct. This pallid conception turned out to give us little more than a name, and at the hands of Mcdougall and Trotter led nowhere in particular except into a curious kind of British Chauvinism. The other approach is that of Freud, who with an oddly limited perspective

contrived to reduce affiliative motives to sexuality—a blunder which even the ancient Greeks, with their distinction between *eros* and *agape*, knew enough to avoid (Allport, 1950).

Taylor's words are:

The Greeks in many ways were much wiser than we are. We are hoping to catch up with them but we haven't yet. The Greeks had four words for our one word "love" ... eros ... agape ... philia ... [storge] (Taylor, 1977).

Each of these four Greek words has a meaning that is distinctive. Beyond these four words there are two other distinctive principles we label "love." This further confuses our understanding and often leads to unhappiness. As a fifth "love," most humans have a need to father or bear a child; this is a distinct need within itself. Sixth, many humans are so confused about "love" they will unconsciously place themselves in distress, many times causing ill feelings from others; yet, it brings forth compassion, which they confuse with the other types of love. This occurs most likely after repeated failures to gain one or more of the other types of love. This is a disastrous path to take because it eventually results in destroying the other types of love.

A brief definition of the six words (principles) is as follows:

1. *Agape*—does not mean affection or sexual arousal. It means I will try to think, speak, and act toward you in the way that is best for you, not for me, regardless of my feelings about you.
2. *Philia*—means affection, delighting to be

in the presence of, a warm feeling, spontaneous and not under the control of one's will.

3. *Storge*—the emotional magnet that draws "blood relatives" together even when agape and philia are absent. The natural bond.

4. *Eros*—sexual interest, arousal, or fulfillment.

5. Placing oneself in distress, usually unconsciously, to get attention and thinking the result is love.

6. The need to father or bear a child which is a need within itself.

We call all of these "love." The word is used to mean so many things it has become almost meaningless. Many people follow Freud's influence without realizing it and reduce all of love to sexuality. Many others reduce all love to philia—"delighting in." How often do we say, "I just love my new car; I love to fish; I love my friend so much; I love a good book"?

As you look at these six words (principles), you will find there is some overlap among them, but the distinctiveness of each is present. Finding the order-understanding of these principles will lead to happier lives. Let us examine in detail each word or principle.

Agape Love Defined
From Vine's *Dictionary of the Greek Language:*

> [Agape] . . . can be known only from the actions it prompts . . . this is not the love of complacency or affection . . . self-will that is self pleasing is the negation of love . . . [it] is not an impulse from the feelings, it does not always run with the natural inclinations. Love [agape] seeks the welfare of all . . . works no ill to any (Vine, 1966).

William Barclay points out:

> Agapan (verb form) has none of the warmth that characterizes *philein*. . . . There is warmth in philein, not in agapan). . . . Agape has to do with the mind: it is not simply an emotion which arises unbidden in our hearts; it is a principle by which we deliberately live. Agape has supremely to do with the will. It is a conquest, a victory, an achievement. . . . The basis of every conceivable right relationship is the love [agape] (Barclay, 1974).

Thayer mentions that agape is not an emotion, while philia (affection) is an emotion, and emotions cannot be commanded. He adds, "From what has been said, it is evident agapao is not, and cannot be, used of sexual love [eros]" (Thayer, 1967).

Kittel's dictionary records:

> In the word *agapan* the Greek finds nothing of the power or magic of eran [sexual love] and little of the warmth of philein. . . . Agapan is a free and decisive act. . . . Agapan must often be translated "to show love"; it is a giving, active love on the other's behalf. . . . It is indeed striking that the substantive agape is almost completely lacking in pre-biblical Greek (Kittel, 1964).

Philia Love Defined

Vine: "Phileo is to be distinguished from agapao in this, that phileo more nearly represents tender affection" (1966).

Thayer: "Phileo denotes an inclination prompted by sense and emotion . . . love as emotion cannot be commanded" (1967).

Barclay, on the noun philia and the verb philein:

There is a lovely warmth about these words. They mean to look on someone with affectionate regard ... best translated "to cherish" ... they have in them all the warmth of real affection ... are beautiful words to express a beautiful relationship ... closeness and affection (1974).

Kittel's dictionary:

Philein/philia ... signifies for the most part the inclination or solicitous love of ... friends for friends ... the warmth of philein. ... It thus denotes natural attraction to those who belong. ... It is then used especially for the love of friends which ... is based on reciprocity (1964).

Storge Defined

Vine refers to natural affection, love of kindred, especially parents for children and children for parents. He also wrote, "a fanciful etymology associates this with the 'stork'" (1966).

Barclay states: "We cannot help loving our kith and kin; blood is thicker than water" (1974).

Eros Love Defined

Kittel: "Eran is passionate love which desires the other for itself.... All the forces of heaven and earth are forces of second rank compared with the one and only supreme power of eros.... Eros seeks in others the fulfillment of its own life hunger" (1964).

Webster's Third New International Dictionary: "Sexual love ... desire ardently ... aspiring self fulfilling love often having a sensuous quality."

Placing Oneself in Distress

This principle, which is called love by many people, is what a person receives by deliberately placing himself in distress. The attention he is given is then called "love." Students, under the stress of an unfinished assignment, will "get sick" to be excused sometimes. The special attention they occasionally receive is pleasurable, and they interpret that as "love" from the teacher. This is true especially if they are deprived of one of the previously mentioned loves to too great an extent. Often then they will persist in maladaptive behavior, reasoning (perhaps unconsciously) that this is the way to be loved. After a while, this behavior is self-defeating, destroying all hope of fulfillment of the other types of love. Unfortunately, husbands, wives, children, parents, employers, employees, and so forth, engage in this practice. Certainly, if one is in distress, and others relieve the distress, that is agape—perhaps even philia love. But that is quite different from placing oneself in distress or purposely bringing distress upon oneself. Over a period of time, the cumulative behavior usually convinces other involved humans which one it is.

When an individual fails in any of the loves to too great an extent, it is possible to choose to act out of hate rather than endure a void of relating to other humans.

H. Thurman gave an address at Boston University on May 4, 1968, in which he said:

> The very spirit of man tends to panic from the desolation of going nameless up and down the streets of other minds where no salutation greets and no friendly recognition makes secure. It is a strange freedom to be adrift in the world of men. . . . It is better to be the complete victim of an anger unrestrained and a wrath which knows no bounds, to be torn

asunder without mercy or battered to a pulp, than to be passed over as if one were not. For here at least one is dealt with, encountered, vanquished, or overwhelmed—but not ignored. To be made anonymous and to give into it is the acquiescence of the heart, it is to live without life, and for such a one, even death is no dying (1968).

Ferenczi said, "They want to love one another, but they don't know how." Frustrated and hungry for a word, a touch, a smile, a shared experience that would satisfy the universal hunger, many people try feverishly to fill the void with semblances of love—activity, popularity, philanthropy, prestige—there are thousands of ways of extracting recognition in lieu of love, none of them satisfactory (Menninger, 1942).

At this point, it is wise to realize that compassion can exist without philia. Have you ever tried to help a compulsive gambler? Again and again you loan him money, but he always gambles it away. Suppose in the beginning you felt warm toward him, you liked him; yet over the months his behavior has chilled the warmth, and now you even feel disgust. He comes to your house, and it is obvious he has been beaten by some loan sharks. You have only disgust, but you realize you could be in his place, so you take him to the emergency room and pay the bill for the stitches.

Compassion, which is a part of agape love, is not synonymous with "affection-warmth-delight to be in the presence of." It is impossible to have affection [philia] for some people who continually bring trouble upon themselves and persistently ask you to "bail them out." You can realize, "But for the grace of God I could be him, repeatedly doing the same acts he is doing."

One can have compassion and philia, also; that is obvious. Compassion is part of agape love. I have had clients in counseling greatly disturbed because they believe they are supposed to have warm feelings about a repeating offender; yet inside of them they feel the emotion of disgust. For some, this false guilt is unbearable. If they understood the above differences, they would not have guilt feelings.

The Need to Father or Bear a Child

Ten years or so ago, I remember reading Rollo May's book *Love and Will*. He hinted strongly, from his personal experiences of working with young males and females, that this must be a need different from the sex act itself. Immediately, it struck me that this has also been my counseling experience. He writes of:

> psychic eruptions which have a curious explosive quality ... some psychic needs more vital, deeper, and more comprehensive than sex. ... We are confronted by the curious situation of *the more birth control, the more illegitimate pregnancies.* ... It is absurd to think this girl, or any girl, gets pregnant simply because she doesn't know better. ... The same is found in our work with men ... impregnating a woman is much more decisive than merely the capacity to have intercourse—but to get some hold on nature, experience a fundamental procreative process, give himself over to some primitive and powerful biological process, partake of some deeper pulsations in the cosmos (May, 1969).

May discusses other motivations that are also present, but it seems to me we must consider the simple behavior of conceiving a baby. How else can we explain all of the couples lined up at the clinics desperately seeking help to conceive a child? Greek mythology and the Hebrew Old Testament (Proverbs 30:15) indicate this need. Some interpret eros to include creativity.

In her book, *Passages*, Gail Sheehy is forced to deal with this need or problem. After quoting studies that yield results of many young women not looking upon having children as important, she writes: "How much of this is their heads talking? Career counselors say that young women students today may *know* that motherhood is no longer a lifetime career, but they still cannot feel that way about it" (Sheehy, 1974).

Now consider the deep confusion, guilt, and trouble that comes from using one word "love" to express six distinct meanings. All therapists could give many examples of people who are mentally ill from this confusion. Probably the great majority of us have suffered from this confusion on this subject.

A wife, full of guilt and the physical signs of anxiety, tells her story:

> I took this job as a secretary, and I have really enjoyed it, but I am so ashamed. There is this man I work for who is so kind, so thoughtful, so much fun to work with. I like—no, I love him—but I love my husband, too. I don't know what I am going to do. I feel so dirty loving two men. I don't mean I have had sex with him; I wouldn't do that. I really love him. Oh! I don't know how to express it. I sound like a high school girl, I am so silly. I can't stand being so sinful. I have been on tranquilizers for three months. I even thought about killing myself.

Variations of the story are endless. Sometimes it is a male; sometimes it takes the turn of separation or divorce.

Most of us have grown up with and have internalized the fairy-tale concept of a "one and only," and he or she will satisfy all my needs if only this true love can be found.

I know of no value system that teaches you are to have *only* a husband or wife to like as a friend, that it is wrong to have any other friends. Is it not possible that the wife quoted here has reduced all philia to eros and she does not distinguish between them? Is she not feeling guilty because she is treating philia the same as eros? Friendship, affection should exist with as many people as possible. That is admirable, desirable, and wonderful. Is it possible she thinks being faithful to one's husband is having *only him* for a friend? She said she has not had sexual intercourse with the other man. This is the value system most Americans have; that is, that sexual intercourse should be restricted to husband and wife. That is fine, and that is my value system, too; but no one person can satisfy the other love needs of agape, philia, and storge. It takes many people. Christianity certainly teaches this.

A man informs you that he is divorcing his wife. The reason: "I no longer love her." What does he mean? Often, he senses that philia is decreasing or absent. I always ask men or women who say this, "Do you think there is anyone in the world with whom philia-affection will *always* be present? Doesn't philia-affection vary with any person from time to time? Usually, they will agree with the implied answers of "no" and "yes." Philia is spontaneous; it comes and goes in varying degrees—that fact must be accepted. It is not the glue that can be depended upon to keep a marriage together. You cannot command or demand it. If you try, you will surely destroy it. Agape is the glue that will keep a marriage or family together. It is the only "love" fully commandable. Eros, I would say, is partly commandable. You can never command a person to feel storge or philia-affection-warmth. By practicing agape love, philia is more likely to develop or to return.

Mothers have "confessed" to me in great distress and the depth of shame of times they have not loved, felt warm toward, their little boy or girl. My response is: "We all have that experience from time to time. Why do you think we should feel warm toward them every minute?" The look of shock and disbelief is astounding. I explain that we should always practice agape, but philia comes and goes. Storge is usually present with your blood relatives. You will want to see them and be with them, even if philia is absent. Have you ever sacrificed to travel many miles at great cost to see Mom and Dad, and then fought with them all the time you were there, or sensed a total void of philia? In spite of that experience, next year you may do it all over again. This illustrates how storge acts like a magnet that pulls blood relatives together—regardless.

Fanshel and Shinn have conducted research and published it in the book, *Children in Foster Care*. They studied 624 children over a five-year span. When the children had regular visits by their natural parents, they showed significant gains: (1) in verbal and non-verbal IQ scores; (2) in emotional adjustment; (3) (a) responsibility and (b) agreeableness, while defiance—hostility and emotionality—tension decreased; and finally, the children's teachers gave them a higher overall positive assessment (1978).

From my own experience as a consultant to child care institutions, I have come to a similar conclusion. The need usually arises for girls (age 15—17) to see their real mother or father. If that desire is thwarted, many will "run" or turn to hostility and even crime. The problem usually surfaces a few years later for boys. I once made the mistake of saying to the houseparents and superintendents: "It would not be best for the child to see either of the real parents. It would be too traumatic, so try to ignore it and do other things with the teenager." It didn't work. I now have changed to say: "This need will surface; before it does, tell the teenagers that if they would like to see their real parent, you will do everything you can to make it possible, and then make sure you do. The teenagers may suffer traumatic effects for a few days or longer after visiting their real parent(s), but it will be better for all concerned in the long run." That usually works. Storge is a powerful need. Many articles are appearing that speak about the depth of this innate need. Fanshel and Shinn stated:

> But the crowning insult—one that goes beyond all of these in its power to debase the human spirit—is for a child to be born without parents who are willing to take care of him. Being cared for in one's own family by one's own parents is a fundamental and almost universal fact of life in almost all societies (1978).

You have probably known children or parents who have been terribly abused both emotionally and physically by blood relatives yet who wept to be with the one who inflicted the torment. That is storge.

Turn the coin over and think how, hopefully, you have had the experience of storge, agape, and philia all being present at the same time with your blood relatives. My mind goes to a winter day. Snow is on the ground, and Sis, Mom, and I are in the kitchen. There is laughter; supper is being cooked; Dad will be home any minute from the Santa Fe railroad shops. The feeling within me now is almost overwhelming. My eyes are moist; a warmth flows throughout my total being. Or, it could be Christmas with my son, daughter, wife, both sets of grandparents present, and again the same emotions flood over me.

How realistic is it to expect agape, philia, and storge to be present every time? It is not realistic. Understanding the differences of the "loves," we can always practice agape. Because it is the only one under control of our mind, it is essential to carrying us through the rough times of family experiences.

A few years ago in one of my senior classes I said: "Do not confer with anyone. Pretend I have just given you $40,000. What would you do with it?" They thought it over, wrote down their answers, and the overwhelming result was to this effect: "I would buy an old farmhouse here in the mountains." We began discussing it. No one could put it into words. No one could explain it until one girl said, "I know why! My dad is lifeless, emotionless, but when he begins talking about the old farm, his eyes light up. I see him as I want him to be. I want it myself. I've noticed others come alive when they talk about the old farmhouse and their experiences." The others generally agreed with enthusiasm. We continued to discuss it and decided it couldn't be boards and nails; therefore, it must be something more—and that was humans relating through working, playing, suffering, depending on each other. It is agape, philia, and storge together.

Returning to storge, Lorraine Dusky wrote in *Newsweek*, October 15, 1979, under the heading "Who Is My Daughter?":

> Somewhere out there is a 13-year-old daughter of mine. Actually, she's another woman's daughter, too. I gave her up for adoption at birth. . . . There are approximately 5 million of us . . . but we do not forget. . . . The experts say that my child, because she is denied her family history, will probably grow up with a sense of distance from other people. Intimacy is likely to be difficult; a vague sense

of unreality may permeate her life. Some psychiatrists have found that a disproportionate number of their patients are adopted. It seems that the psychological connection to one's roots is critical. Inevitable curiosity sets in as soon as you tell a child he or she is adopted, and subsequent secrecy only poisons the adoptive relationship.

Dusky then quotes a young woman who said, "The way it is now . . . there is something missing from my life." Dusky continues:

> Having spoken to a great many natural mothers over the last eight years, I believe that the desire to find out what happens to our children is universal, or nearly so. The available data bear this out. The bond of birth is in our genes (1980).

Truly, the Greeks had a word for it—storge. An article by Cherin Poovey about an adoptee, Carla Carroll, illustrates the strength of storge from the adoptee's view.

> But for all of her 20 years, Mrs. Carroll has lacked the one piece she feels would make her life's puzzle complete: the identity of her natural mother . . . she insists, she has the right to know who gave her life. . . . The desire to know who her natural mother is is always with her. . . . "Even if it's not meant to be [that I find her], that doesn't mean that I can't keep searching. . . . I would like to think that my natural mother is a good person and that we would want to keep in touch if she were found," she said. "I'd be extremely relieved" (1980).

Storge is the force that makes us search for our "roots." This is the reason many feel "rootless" and "unanchored."

Adoptees and their adopted parents must accept this need and not feel threatened by it. By definition, they cannot ever have storge, but agape and philia can be so enriching for all concerned; however, to try to force storge to exist between non-blood relatives is impossible and disastrous and can destroy agape and philia. Contact between children and their real parents must be encouraged, and laws should be changed to make it possible. We are made that way.

We now have a framework (an order) by which we can explain incest and, therefore, help to overcome it.

If a father has been raised to internalize all love as eros-sex, he has no concept of storge. If he also has an unsatisfactory sex life with his wife, it is likely that when his little girl reaches the age of puberty and begins to turn to Daddy to express and to receive storge, he will perceive it as sexual. The outcome can easily be incest. Of course, it also occurs between mothers and sons. The reduction of all love to only one of the six kinds of love will lead to trouble. We must learn the six principles.

It is easy to understand how those who reduce all love to sex can end up in a homosexual relationship because they do not know what philia is and that it is not sexual.

Eros Love

We now have a framework by which we can understand how eros between the same two people may one time be an ecstatic experience and another time be "blah." We all have experienced this. Probably females have the blah experience more than males because of the hormonal difference. It is not an easy

task to understand the basic physical difference of
need for sexual intercourse between male and female.
The following quotations point out that for a male accustomed to sexual activity, the average need is once
every three days, approximately, while the female has
the need only once every thirteen days, approximately.
This is true at the physical hormonal level; yet the other
aspects of sexual stimulation, as well as causes of
frustration, are pointed out.

> Heterosexuality . . . emerges as a distant enti-
> ty at the time of puberty, matures during
> adolescence, and operates as the primary
> sociosexual affectional system for most
> adults. . . . Sex is a complex and pervasive
> force that has a biological basis but can func-
> tion properly (or be understood adequately)
> only in the context of affectional networks
> and life as a whole. . . .
>
> Human sexual behavior, however,
> is so profoundly influenced by learning ex-
> periences that it is extremely difficult to sort
> out the effects of sex hormones on the sex
> drive. . . .
>
> Deprivation of sex hormones
> through removal of the ovaries or testes has
> little or no effect upon the sex drive in adults.
>
> Administration of female sex hor-
> mones to males seems to diminish the sex
> drive in some instances; administration of
> male sex hormones seems to enhance the sex
> drive in some women. . . .
>
> Studies have shown . . . that there
> are predictable variations in the frequency of
> intercourse during the menstrual cycle in
> large groups of women, with peaks occurring
> at midcycle and just before menstruation. . . .

Some studies show that the period of maximum progesterone secretion is usually one of the least sexual activity. On the other hand there is some evidence that the androgens secreted by the adrenal glands play a role in the sex drives of women, and surgical removal of the adrenal glands has a more predictable effect on the libido than does the removal of the ovaries. Women who receive androgenic hormones for medical reasons also report dramatic increases in sexual desire while under treatment (Katchadourian and Lunde, 1972).

Eroticism in man is a complex of signs and signals including physiomatic signs from the reproductive system, behavioral gestures of premating and mating endeavors and language messages about sexual sensations, imagery and expectancy. ... It is impossible at the present state of scientific knowledge to identify the full variety of related forms of sex hormones that are functionally active in the body or to estimate their quantity. ... Loss of only the ovaries and ovarian hormones had no definite adverse effect on sexual drive, activity and response, but all these were diminished in most of the women after their adrenals also had been removed. The adrenals secrete some estrogen, but large amounts of androgen .. androgen is the hormone of eroticism in men and women ... many men for whom estrogen is prescribed report great diminution or total abolition of sexual drive and activity (Money, 1961).

Estrogen, a steroid compound, is the principal agent for the first half of the menstrual cycle. As in the male the generation and hormonal apparatus is largely neutral until puberty. . . . Each month one or more . . . ova . . . begins to become a functioning, fertilizable ovum. It becomes surrounded by a group of nest cells. . . . This becomes a large enough aggregate to be a temporary endocrine gland. The cells secrete . . . estrogen . . . the total amount made in a year is 120 m.g. This is roughly 1/3 the weight of a single ordinary aspirin tablet . . . a woman produces about 2/3 as much male hormone (androgen) as a man. . . . It is a complex machine all built to basically serve the need for reproduction of the species. Its end function may be hopelessly confused by the social dictates of the culture. . . . The basic nature is there and its proponent needs must be met.

The sexual drive in the female is made up of the same elements found in the male. Arousal of the drive will lead to tumescence . . . the female may arrive at reproduction behavior by one or more of three routes.

First, the cycle itself dictates the occurrence of visceral-originated arousal. This is probably the fundamental method by which the race survives, since it accentuates the drive, or the sexual receptivity, of even the female who lacks either of the other two aspects. This accounts for the common occurrence of the sexually frigid woman with a full complement of off-spring. . . . At near mid-cycle the graafian follicle is ripe, full of estrogen for sudden release. When it is released, the female activity goes up, the temperature rises, and the uterus and tubes increase in motion. A modern pelvic congestion ensues. The sensory impulses from the turgid, pulsing, contracting female tubular structures are conveyed to the diencephalon ... the female may respond by overt behavior but more likely will have spontaneous erection of the clitoris (similar to erection of the penis in the male), labia minora, or the nipples as the response from the thalmic area. ... She will be more receptive to the advancing male.

The second route to sexual arousal in the female ... the responsiveness of the erotogenic zones. As in the male, the erogenous zones are primarily the mucocutaneous junction tissues. The clitoris in its small area concentrates the same friction-sensitive nerve endings as the whole corona of the glans penis; the labia minora and the brief rim of the vagina introitus are triggered to fill and erect at a slight touch. The mouth is conditioned and the salivary glands are active. The lips are ready to seek out pressure and contact with the other mouth and tongue. The nipples and aroelae become acutely sensitive to touch and movement. All the sensory modalities of the male are here in quantity. For many females, arousal occurs only after exploration and stimulation of these areas. Almost certainly, all are preconditioned at ovulation time by the visceral response (Trainer, 1965).

In our present time, false values internalized by many wives (and some husbands) cause them to reject many of the feelings that flow from their sexual nature. Sometimes this leads to denial, repression, hostility, or guilt as they experience these sexual sensations. In their confusion and frustration, they quite often express it against the husband, blaming him for what they perceive as their "bad," "unladylike," or even sinful reactions to him. Wives and husbands must have a value system that permits full enjoyment of sexual arousal, foreplay, exploration, and sexual intercourse without any "bad" feelings.

Returning to Trainer's words:

> The third route to sexual behavior in the female is the uniquely human route ... [shared with the male]. It is the cerebral cortically engendered drive and depends on imagery and memory. The imagery derives from the memory of sight and its correlative, the prehensile [grasping] hand; from hearing; from perception of a loved one's odors; from taste and the sensation of body flavors. These are wrapped in the manifold memory pattern of the beloved. Their pleasant emergence into consciousness by some small evocative event may quickly activate all the mating behavior, fire off visceral responses, and trigger the erogenous zones. This is a human characteristic unshared by even the primates. In both man and woman it will be the basis for the very wide, essentially non-reproductive variety of love play common to man and woman throughout a score of socially different cultures. ...

> The male repetition rate is about 72 hours (Trainer, 1965).

We must recognize the wide individual variation as to sexual need, but there is a basic difference between the male and the female. The other two routes to sexual stimulation described by Trainer become very important. The wife must permit, even encourage, the other two routes; and the husband must develop and become proficient in exercising them if there is to be mutual sexual satisfaction. Beyond the two routes, agape and philia love must be expressed consistently and congruently throughout the day and night to facilitate the two routes to sexual arousal. This gives more practical meaning to Katchadourian and Lunde's statement, "Sex is a complex and pervasive force that has a biological basis but can function properly (or be understood adequately) only in the context of affectional networks and life as a whole" (1972). A common error of males is ignorance of the relatedness of all the types of love (except storge) to sexual love.

Likewise, it is extremely important for the social and moral institutions (church, schools, family, etc.) to instill the proper values within each generation so that husbands and wives can initiate, respond fully, and completely give themselves without reserve to each other.

General frustration and specific sexual frustration can result from: (1) ignorance of one's own sexual nature; (2) ignorance of the sexual nature of the opposite sex; or (3) internalized false values. Shere Hite collected statements from females expressing this sexual unfulfillment which she labeled "vaginal ache":

> What happens is this: sometimes building up to and just at the moment of orgasm there is intense pleasure/pain feeling deep inside the vagina, something like a desire to be entered or touched inside, or just an exquisite sensation of pleasure, which we call "vaginal ache." ... Some women perceive this feeling as hollow, empty, and unpleasant, while others find it intensely pleasurable.... For

most women . . . the penis seems to "soothe" and diffuse the feeling, so it depends on whether you prefer to feel the sensation or not (1971).

Past experiences and internalized values determine one's feeling as pleasurable or not and the sex act as pleasurable or not.

Dr. Stephen Neiger describes the reaction to the lack of orgasm as uncomfortable congestion which may result in back and/or pelvic pain (1973).

Dr. Joseph Trainer writes:

Those who fail to reach orgasm similarly fail to go through a reasonably rapid resolution stage. This woman will be restless, tense, dissatisfied or unsatisfied, and her initially agreeable pelvic congestion may turn to pelvic discomfort or pain. She will be unable to sleep or read and may lie awake for a long time (1965).

Drs. Abraham and Hannah Stone describe actual orgasm deficiency:

If her sexual impulse is not very strong, or if she is aroused only to a slight degree, the absence of the orgasm will hardly have any harmful effects. On the other hand, if she has been very much stimulated, the failure to reach a climax may leave her in a state of frustration which may prove physiologically and emotionally disturbing. During erotic excitation there is a marked local congestion of the sexual organs, as well as a general physical and emotional tension. With the completion of the act, if the climax is reached, there is a gradual release, or detumescence, followed by a sense of fulfillment and relaxation. In the absence of an orgasm, however, the relief is not complete and the woman may remain for some time in an unsatisfied and restless condition. Repeated experiences of this kind may eventually lead to various physical or emotional disturbances (1968).

Concerning sexual frustration in the male, Hinsie and Campbell record Freud's words:

When the instinctual urge cannot be handled normally by the subject, he may summon all his energies to the satisfaction of the urge, disregarding the mores of his surroundings. Or he may regress, that is the frustrated libido [sex drive energy] may be withdrawn from objects in reality and take refuge in the life of phantasy where it creates new wish-formations and reanimates the vestiges of earlier forgotten ones (1970).

Trainer writes:

In terms of energetics, sex hormones must unquestionably be the most powerful substance made. . . . This device [penis] makes its owner single-mindedly anxious to use it; it gives him an incomparable sense of satisfaction when he does; its use leaves him with a degree of relaxation otherwise unattainable (1965).

A list of possible maladaptive reactions resulting from sexual frustration but not restricted to sexual frustration only would include:

1. Literally fighting in thoughts, words, actions, verbally and/or nonverbally, including rape and murder.
2. Literally trembling in thoughts, words, or actions verbally and/or nonverbally, in-

cluding epilepsy that is functionally caused.
3. Literally fleeing in thoughts, words, or actions verbally or nonverbally, including amnesia and suicide.
4. Resorting to defense mechanisms.
5. Resorting to psycho-physiological illnesses.
6. Resorting to conversion reactions.
7. Resorting to mind-altering substances (drugs), including alcohol.
8. Resorting to sexual deviations.

George Vaillant's research work with 268 men reveals how mentally healthy people react to sexual frustration or any need frustration. One or more of the following are used:

1. Altruism: Vicarious but constructive and instinctually gratifying service to others ... provides real, not imaginary, benefit to others ... leaves the person ... at least partly gratified.
2. Humor: Overt expression of ideas and feelings without individual discomfort or immobilization and without unpleasant effect on others ... humor lets you call a spade a spade ... humor permits one to bear and yet to focus upon what is too terrible to be borne. ...
3. Suppression: The conscious or semiconscious decision to postpone paying attention to a conscious impulse of conflict ... includes looking for silver linings, minimizing acknowledged discomfort, employing a stiff upper lip, and deliberately postponing but not avoiding.
4. Anticipation: Realistic anticipation of or planning for future inner discomfort ... includes goal directed but not overly careful planning or worrying, premature but realistic

affective anticipation ... and the conscious utilization of insight. ...

5. Sublimation: Indirect or attenuated expression of instincts without either adverse consequences or marked loss of pleasure.

It includes both expressing aggression through pleasurable games, sports, and hobbies ... instincts are channeled rather than dammed or diverted. ... In sublimation, feelings are acknowledged, modified and directed toward a relatively significant person or goal so that modest instinctual satisfaction results (1977).

Masturbation to ejaculation or orgasm is a specific form of sublimation. This is a "touchy" subject because of one's values, morals, and church teachings being involved. It is not wise to use it if one's conscience condemns it. Research shows that a great percentage of males masturbate, and a smaller percentage of females do, probably because of the physical hormonal differences between the two sexes. Most religions do not condemn masturbation if it is not accompanied by lust. The only acceptable definition of "lust" that I know of is "giving the consent of the mind to have and/or phantasizing sexual intercourse with a person not your husband or wife" (Rigdon, 1978). Here the opposite of lust while masturbating would be to vividly imagine in the future or to recall a pleasurable time of sexual intercourse with your husband or wife and to masturbate to orgasm or ejaculation. Hinsie and Campbell define "masturbation" as:

Direct self-manipulation of the genitals, most commonly by the hand, accompanied by phantasies that are usually of a recognizable sexual nature, and having as its aim the discharge of sexual excitation. "Psychic masturbation" is also recognized, where phantasy alone is sufficient to effect sexual discharge without any direct physical manipulation. The masturbatory act then has two aspects—form (the physical manipulations) and content (the nature of the accompanying or provoking phantasy) (1970).

Too many people don't recognize that it is normal for the need of sex to make itself known in the mind and body, and that it is not sinful. It is essential to differentiate the need of sex from temptation, lust, and the sexual act. Temptation is treated by some as sinful—something to feel guilty about. This is an example of false religious teaching causing mental disturbance.

Returning to the subject of frustrated sexual drives of males and females, the male *almost always* needs ejaculation for satisfaction. That does not seem to be true for the female, but that does not mean it is unimportant. The husband and wife have a responsibility to satisfy each other sexually. Extremes of selfishness must be avoided. Extremes of uninterested passivity, usually on the female's part ("Hurry up and get it over with; I'll permit you to enter me, but don't expect me to assist it or move on your penis.") must likewise be avoided. Normal people, without false guilt and without false inhibitions, derive pleasure from giving sexual pleasure as well as receiving it. Because of the physical hormonal differences (female once every thirteen days as compared with male once every three days), it will fall on the female to *provide* pleasure more often. Mature females, well adjusted sexually, do not view this as a burden or a terrible thing. They will take pride in bringing sexual pleasure to the husband. Likewise, mature husbands will understand the physical difference and be more understanding and less demanding sexually.

When sexual problems become too great, they must be communicated. For many couples, this is extremely difficult, probably because of false religious teaching, Puritanism, and fairy tales that make us internalize "romantic sexual love" as something that cannot be discussed without ruining it—taking all the mystery and excitement out of it. That extreme must be overcome. To do so will take time, patience, tact, and courage. Some couples can begin only by reading about it as individuals, not even reading it together. However, the goal is verbal-nonverbal communication as to what pleases each sexually. He is active in the sexual act; she is active in guiding, moving, rewarding, etc. Many males lose their self-respect and may even become unfaithful to or impotent with their wives because of the repeated lack of verbal and nonverbal response and/or initiation on the part of the wife. Lack of self-respect-worth is the main cause of frigidity or impotence. Chapter 5 will deal with self-respect in general. On the present subject, the goal is thoughtful, considerate, compassionate sexual communication.

There is another problem that has been experienced in counseling sessions with patients often enough that it needs to be mentioned and clarified. Many young mothers suffer false guilt from experiencing varying degrees of sexual excitement while nursing their infants. I have counseled mothers who were unable to continue nursing their babies because of this false guilt. Some are guilt-ridden to the point of suicide. Some express that they are "full of incest," that they "hate such an evil inside of them." Mothers must learn that *most* women experience some degree of sexual excitement, some even to orgasm, while nursing their babies, and that is perfectly normal. There is no reason for feeling guilty.

Eiger and Olds write:

> The hormone oxytocin surges through a woman's body during orgasm, during childbirth, and during lactation. It is this hormone

that causes the uterus to contract and the nipples to become erect. Oxytocin is also the stimulus for the milk-ejection reflex, and nursing mothers commonly report that milk spurts from their breasts when they reach orgasm. . . . Unfortunately, those women who do experience sexual arousal during nursing are apt to feel guilty—so guilty that they may wean their babies early and refuse to nurse future children. In our society sexual feelings are supposed to stay in their place—to come out of hiding only when a culturally determined suitable partner is present. Yet, we are sexual beings and our sexual feelings spin a thread that runs through the fabric of our entire lives. It is truly a shame that more women who realize sexual stimulation from breastfeeding cannot relax and enjoy these pleasurable sensations (1972).

Another common problem is the attitude of many males which is brought to sexual intercourse from their social, cultural heritage. Males, very early in life, hear four-letter words which stand for sexual intercourse but are used as an expression of hate, violence, ridicule, and derision toward others. The accumulation of these experiences warp many male minds until they think of violence, pain, hate, and belittling whenever they engage in sex with their wife. Think of the inward contradictions, confusions, guilt, and frustration if a male has internalized sex as violence and yet at the same instant has affection for his wife in the sexual act. This accounts for some men who can only function satisfactorily with a "whore" and who are impotent with their wives.

This internalization of sex as hostility is furthered by the magazines in the bookstores which depict females threatened with knives, guns, broken bottles, with terror in their eyes, and at the same time sexual overtones are present—breasts exposed, panties being torn off, etc. Add to this the common ignorance of most males which still exists (contrary to public opinion) who do not realize the necessity of time and foreplay to properly arouse the female sexually so that entrance by the penis into the vagina is not painful. This occurs too often, and immediately they reconnect and affirm sex as an attack, painful, and brutal. The female, also, has often internalized the same unfortunate attitude. Now we can understand how sex is never as it should be for many couples. How unfortunate!

Earlier, sexual dysfunctions were referred to as a result of frustrated sexual needs. A fairly complete list and brief definition would be:

> 1. Impotence: Inability of the male to obtain or maintain an erection of the penis for satisfactory sexual intercourse for him or her.
> 2. Premature ejaculation: The ejection of the semen by the male before or too soon after his penis enters her vagina.
> 3. Frigidity: The female too often having very little or no pleasure in sexual stimulation, intercourse.
> 4. Dyspareunia: Painful or difficult sexual intercourse. (Usually this is not organic in nature; only about 5 to 10 percent of the time is there an organic cause.)
> 5. Vaginismus: Painful, involuntary spasms of the vaginal muscles for the female (usually functional, not organic in nature).

Generally, sexual dysfunction may be defined as any impairment of sexual function—not functioning sexually to give or receive sexual satisfaction.

Sexual dysfunctions must not be confused

with sexual deviations which are defined as "sexual behavior which is markedly at variance with the generally accepted forms of sexual activity" (Osol, ed., 1972). A few examples and definitions of sexual deviations are:

> 1. Fetishism: Sexual arousal and gratification only from inanimate objects.
> 2. Pedophilia: Sexual relations between an adult and a child.
> 3. Transvestism: Sexual gratification from wearing the clothes and adopting the role of the opposite sex.
> 4. Voyeurism: Inability to obtain sexual satisfaction except by looking at nude people.
> 5. Sadism: Sexual gratification from inflicting pain upon one's sexual partner.
> 6. Masochism: Sexual gratification from experiencing pain personally.
> 7. Exhibitionism: Sexual gratification from exposing one's genitals.
> 8. Incest: Sexual relations between close relatives.
> 9. Bestiality: Human to beast sexual relations.
> 10. Rape: Sexual intercourse with another person (not the marriage partner), without that person's consent, by force.

Human sexuality is indeed complex, but it is not hopelessly confusing. It includes not only the biological, physical, hormonal basis, but also values, social norms, cultural dictates, religious principles, and the unique individual differences.

Daniel Day Williams wrote:

> For what is communicated through sexual behavior is never fully determined by sexuality or the sexual act itself ... for man the

organic urges and acts are never detached from the search for meaning. The search may be successful or destructive, wholesome or corrupted. It is always the self's search for belonging through communication with another. This is why sexual attraction by itself is such a fleeting, superficial and undependable indicator of what sexuality really is. There is an implicit question in all human sexual attraction: "What use will you make of me? What do you want and expect of me, and are you exploiting me or loving me?" ... The human body with its gestures and expression, its beauty or ugliness, its reflection of spirit in the human face, its postures of tenderness or hostility, its acts of intimacy and separation, articulates the language of the self. Alfred North Whitehead brilliantly defines the human body as the primary field of human expression. So every bodily action becomes symbolically the incarnation of a human attitude in the whole gamut from ecstatic fulfillment to boredom and despair....Men cannot employ the language [the act] of sex without consequences any more than women can. An exploitative sexual relationship stupefies the spirit. Its result is insensitivity to the depth and glory of personal communication (1968).

Agape and Eros

To agape-love your mate in sexual intercourse requires an understanding of his/her sexual nature. The male-female differences and his/her individual likes/dislikes must be understood and respected. Inhibitions must be discarded, but this takes time and patience by both parties. Each must be willing to change. Verbal and nonverbal communication that is open and honest, yet tactful and considerate, is necessary.

Agape must be practiced in all other areas and times of life for the application of agape in sexual foreplay and sexual intercourse to be perceived by the other as sincere, genuine, and meaningful.

Agape in sexuality is talking, looking, touching, caressing, responding as you would want your mate to do unto you if you were he or she.

Quoting again from Daniel Day Williams:

> The will to belong, we have said, is fundamental in human existence. . . . Human belonging does not mean physical possession alone; indeed the language of possession violates the spirit of belonging.
>
> The will to belong is the will to communicate, to express oneself and to find a response. Thus the search for belonging becomes in large measure a search for language which will open the way to speaking and hearing. This is why verbal behavior is so closely linked with the emotional dynamics of the self and especially with sexuality. . . . Eros, philia, and agape . . . each has its contribution to make to the fullness of love. But balance and proportion between the different constituents of love is not automatic, and is usually attained only with that persistent effort which is one of the joys and responsibilities which lovers share. . . . No person is ever fulfilled in the family alone and no romanticism about love should obscure the fact. . . . We have to find a union of love in its obligation to those with whom our lives are immediately bound; and love which calls upon each to become a creative member of the full society. . . . Pretensions of absolute righteousness

are as offensive to love as positive unrighteousness (1968).

Eros and Philia

One of the most tragic human faults is to reach a point in living that one cannot or will not express philia-affection when it is experienced toward another individual. Even worse are those poor souls who refuse to allow the feeling of affection to arise within them. They actively push it back into the unconscious. These are people who are alive but are not living. Their spirit is dead. There is no gleam in their eye nor spring in their step. They are to be pitied the most. When philia is genuinely, spontaneously experienced concomitant with sexuality, it enriches sexuality to a peak experience of oceanic feelings that overwhelm the individual with tidal waves of joy—pure ecstasy.

Philia cannot be forced, but when it is felt, it must be expressed verbally and nonverbally. Philia present with eros is the best definition of romantic love—the great mysterious force that all normal people long for and seek after. There are many reasons why people repress and refuse to express philia. Almost always it is because of unfortunate past experiences of neglect, ridicule, rejection, being taken advantage of, etc., when they did sincerely, genuinely, openly give philia to another human. The other person may have been father, mother, other family member, boyfriend, girl friend, teacher, or friend. Philia is necessary in many different situations. It must never be restricted to sexual encounters or treated synonymously with eros, but when it is present with eros, then both are magnified and enjoyed many times over.

Rejection of philia in any aspect of a relationship, repeated over and over, may cause a person to repress philia in all relationships, including sexual ones. A child who naturally (and it *is* natural) gives philia to a father who cannot or will not reciprocate may eventually stifle all philia to any other humans. An adolescent girl who fully gives philia to a boy, and then perceives she is being treated only as a sexual object by him with no philia in return, may harden her feelings to the point that philia is never permitted to surface again. How tragic for her and all others with whom she comes in contact later on in life.

E. Fromm said, "To live at all requires faith, courage, trust, and perseverance . . . it is a 'chancy' thing."

C. S. Lewis said, "To love at all is to be vulnerable. Love anything, and your heart will certainly be wrung and possibly broken. Yet to refuse to love is the greatest of tragedies" (1960).

Five

Self-Esteem

The fourth need, self-esteem, is also referred to as self-respect, self-worth, self-regard, or human dignity. How it is labeled is not nearly as important as understanding what it is and how it is fulfilled. Self-esteem is often confused with conceit, and this is probably the reason so many people refuse to fulfill it, systematically depriving themselves of it until they are emotionally malnourished into a condition which we call depression. Depression is usually caused by unfulfilled self-esteem.

Before it becomes serious enough to label depression, we describe it as feeling "blue," "down," "always tired," "the spark is gone," "hopeless," or "why try?" When it goes beyond depression, it often results in suicide. Since our societal-cultural norms do not permit a male to express the before-mentioned characteristics of unfulfilled self-esteem, the male often indicates it by staying away, anger, irritableness, not talking, being short tempered, snapping at people, emotionally or physically abusing the family, etc.

Frieda Fromm Reichman writes, "Since he lives in a society and in a culture where the display of fear or anxiety is coexistent with an alleged or real decrease of prestige or self-respect, he may tend to convert his anxiety into anger" (1967). Because the need of self-esteem is a part of the order within us, any time we do not know the order or the order is broken, the result is anxiety, as well as depression, which are at opposite ends of the emotional pole. Think of a rubber band—limp, lifeless. Now stretch it until it quivers and almost breaks; sometimes it does break. This is a theory that explains people labeled manic-depressive who suffer extreme swings of mood from too high to too low and back and forth.

J. F. Kauffman defined self-esteem as, "A basic sense of one's own value, not vanity or false pride, but a proper sense of self regard . . . a conviction one is a self worth being" (1968). He further commented, "Clinicians are well aware in a general way that many of the disturbed patients who come to them for treatment feel themselves to be incompetent and socially rejected" (1968). A. Adler wrote, "Mentally healthy people have to have a satisfactory view of self and a view of cooperation not opposition to one's social and physical environment" (Ansbacher, 1969). That (like most statements) could be taken to extremes where it becomes wrong; but not taken to extremes, it is true. W. Glasser states: "Equal to the importance of the need for love is the need that we are worthwhile both to ourselves and to others. . . . If we do not fulfill our need to feel worthwhile, we will suffer as acutely as when we fail to love and be loved" (1965).

W. James wrote:

A man ... with powers that have uniformly brought him success with place and wealth and friends and fame, is not likely to be visited by the morbid diffidences and doubts about himself which he had when he was a boy, whereas he who has made one blunder after another and still lies in middle life among the failures at the foot of the hill is liable to grow ... with self distrust and to shrink from trials with which his powers can really cope (Coopersmith, 1968).

Hinsie and Campbell write, "Pathologic loss of self-esteem is characteristic of clinical depression" (1970).

When people violate their conscience by doing something they feel they should not do or by not doing something they feel they should do, they suffer guilt which keeps self-esteem from being fulfilled. It is common for humans to express it with the following words: "I feel dirty"; "My skin is crawling"; "I don't like to see my reflection"; "I feel sinful, bad—terrible"; "I'm awful." Glasser, referring to this principle, writes:

Even a child knows the difference between right and wrong behavior and he is frustrated when receiving love for behavior that he knows is wrong. This keeps him from feeling worthwhile. To be worthwhile we must maintain a satisfactory standard of behavior. To do so we must learn to correct ourselves when we do wrong and to credit ourselves when we do right (1965).

Too many people confuse this "credit ourselves" with conceit. How unfortunate! The Bible teaches that when people refuse to give in to a temptation they "will have reason for boasting [glorying, rejoicing, in different translations] in regard to himself alone" (Galatians 6:4). I hasten to mention that the same Scripture passages condemn conceit (bragging to others). However, it is interesting that the Scriptures approve "crediting self" or "in regard to himself alone" while condemning conceit-bragging. We need to learn the lesson of Proverbs 27:2: "Let another praise you, and not your own mouth; a stranger, and not your own lips."

All therapists, like myself, have had several patients who could not, would not, let anyone compliment them because they treated that as conceit and, therefore, sin. I liken these people to humans, who while literally starving to death, are offered food; but they adamantly refuse it and die. Too many humans are dying for lack of self-esteem; yet, they think they are holy for doing it. It is a strange phenomenon that one can liken to anorexia nervosa; in fact, I label this anorexia nervosa of the need of self-esteem.

The need of self-esteem, just as all other needs, is circular in nature. One may feel useful, worthwhile, happy, and energetic, but over a period of time, one uses it up. Nothing has to happen. One must continually replenish self-esteem just as one would eat again after the body has used up the previous meal. Also, self-esteem is usually fulfilled in relationship to others. We are dependent, but we are not helpless. When people verbally and/or nonverbally prize, praise, honor, respect us, we have our need for self-respect replenished.

To summarize and oversimplify what humans must do to respect self, and to have others respect them:

1. Produce something (a service, product, etc.) that others need or want.
2. Live up to one's values, standards.
3. Discipline self.

Producing Something

Burt Shater insists that "Occupational experiences which confirm a person's competence are the most important, even more important than finding a group role, a sex role, or a world view" (Sheehy, 1974). Sheehy also quotes Erikson: "In general, it is the inability to settle on an occupational identity which most disturbs young people" (1974). She says, "Most theorists agree that more than anything else, it is successful work experience that helps a young person resolve the conflicts of dependency and establish an independent identity" (1974).

This was my personal experience growing up, and I have used it successfully in counseling young people. As one grows older, the *type* of occupation and the skills of the person become very important. One wishes to do what he/she is capable of doing and also to do that which gains respect from other human beings. To clarify "respect," look at its meaning and then its opposites. To respect means to consider worthy of esteem, to regard or treat with honor or deference, to value, to consider, deem, observe, revere, venerate, hold in high estimation, bestow dignity, courtesy, appreciate, value, prize, praise. Think of the opposites and apply them emotionally to yourself to fully grasp the significance of this need and its dependency on others to fulfill. Some antonyms: disregard, ignore, violate, disdain, despise, show contempt, scorn, look down on.

Successful marriages depend to a large extent on mates treating each other with respect—valuing each other. Success in rearing children is largely dependent upon communicating verbally and nonverbally from the parents to each child, "You have worth." Success in business-industrial relationships—*all relationships*—depend to a large extent on the mutual need of self-esteem and human dependency on others for fulfillment. Humans must, if at all possible, produce something other humans need or want. All of us must practice communicating respect to others who do this. It is a reciprocal process by which all humans profit and are made happier and have meaning added to existence.

The female in our time is going through a difficult period. Recently, society has devalued having children and raising children. So the woman has this innate need to bear children but receives numerous small communications of disdain for it. This is the driving force that causes most mothers to find an occupation outside the home. She doesn't know why an occupation fulfills her because, generally speaking, she (like many of us) has not understood this basic emotional need of self-esteem. This understanding also gives us the basic framework to understand why many females go through depression at menopause. They are the ones who unconsciously have internalized that having children is the highest and *only* way that "I am unique," "me," "different from my husband." It is "the one thing he cannot do that I can." Of course, depression sets in if such women find it necessary to have surgery that absolutely ends this possibility of bearing a child. This also explains why a man often suffers deep depression if he is impotent. In the unconscious mind of the male, well-being and potency become so related that depression for other reasons may cause impotency. This basic principle of producing something that other humans need or want, in order to fulfill one's self-esteem, helps explain Vaillant's research findings. He found that mentally healthy men cope or adapt to instinctual or need deprivation by altruistic acts toward others, which he explains as "vicarious but constructive and instinctually gratifying service to others ... real not imaginary benefit to others" (1977). When one does this consistently and congruently, others appreciate, prize, praise, honor the one doing it. Both benefit, and this is a rational way to cope with deprivations in one's own life.

Living up to One's Values—Morals

Somehow over the years many have been led to believe that you can violate your conscience without adverse consequences. Experience teaches the opposite. An exception would be the sociopath; but remember that an exception does not destroy the rule, and who would recommend becoming a sociopath?

Freedman, Kaplan, and Sadock write, "Guilt begins with parental disapproval and becomes internalized as conscience in the course of superego development. Guilt has normal psychological and social functions, but special intensity or absence of guilt characterizes many mental disorders, such as depression and antisocial personality" (1972). This excellent statement warns about extremism on this point. Society could not exist without the internal restraints which guilt places on us.

In the past and present some have suggested removing all restraints. If we did achieve this, crime, rape, robbery, murder would make life impossible. Perhaps this is why we have our present problems of crime. On the other hand, all therapists have had patients whose consciences were too strict. There are some who, if they see a drunk person, react as if they are guilty of drunkenness, etc. Special intensity, too strict a conscience, perfectionism, can lead to anxiety and/or depression. There has to be a balance for happiness in everyday living. Extremes must be avoided. By living up to our standards, values, morals we have our need of self-esteem fulfilled.

Disciplining of Self

This principle is a part of living up to one's values; yet it is different enough to deserve special attention. Probably, it flows from the discipline we have received from those who raised us. Again, the two extremes can be disastrous. The two extremes are: everything must be done now, no matter how small, or everything is put off until tomorrow. Stanley Coopersmith and his associates have done excellent research on self-esteem with boys.

> We found, not very surprisingly, that youngsters with a high degree of self esteem are active, expressive individuals who tend to be successful both academically and socially. ... In contrast, the boys with low self esteem presented a picture of discouragement and depression. They felt isolated, unlovable, incapable of expressing or defending themselves and too weak to confront or overcome their deficiencies. They were fearful of angering others and shrank from exposing themselves to notice in any way.... We found no consistent relationship between self esteem and physical attractiveness, height, the size of the boy's family, early trauma, breast or bottle-feeding in infancy or the mother's principal occupation.... Even more surprising, our subjects' self esteem depended only weakly, if at all, on family position or income level.
>
> Summarizing what was responsible for high self esteem they mention "their sub-

ject's *treatment* and their *achievements*." Important antecedents were parent's *interest* in the boy's welfare, *concern* about their companions, *availability* for *discussion* of the boy's problem and participation in congenial joint activities. Parents of high self esteem children proved to be *less permissive.* . . . They demanded high standards of behavior and were *strict* and *consistent* in enforcement of the rules. Yet their discipline was by no means harsh (1968).

If parents are extremely harsh, children may rebel to no self-discipline or follow the same harshness toward themselves. All have experienced the pendulum theory in self and in observation of others. Extremes often beget extremes. Perhaps this explains why children of alcoholics may be extreme in their bitterness against alcohol or, on the other hand, may become alcoholics. The happy medium is difficult to obtain in such a case, whether it is in politics, religion, financial responsibility, alcoholism, or self-esteem.

In my own life, I know that if I continually procrastinate grading papers, emotions such as bitterness, short temper, edginess, etc., begin to build within me. If other small tasks accumulate and I lack the self-discipline to do them, my emotional state deteriorates. On the other hand, if I "keep up," I am much happier.

"Mentally healthy people have to have a satisfactory view of self and a view of cooperation not opposition to one's social and physical environment" (Ansbacher, 1969).

Notice Figure 6.

If we consistently, congruently do the three previous things: (1) produce something needed by others; (2) live up to our standards, values, morals; and (3) discipline self, we will experience the fulfillment of

Figure 6
Self-Depreciation or Self-Respect or Conceit

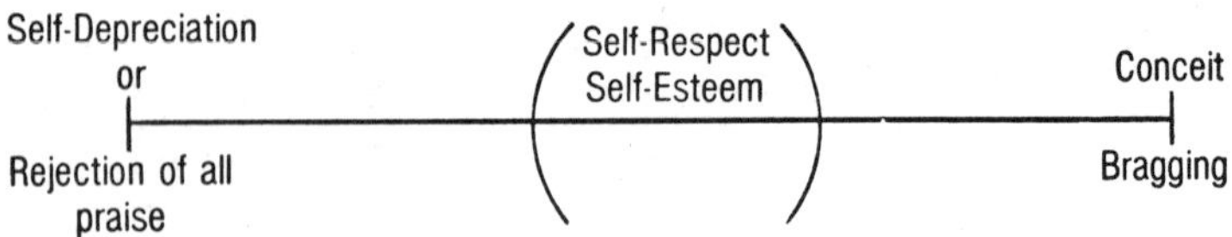

self-esteem *if* we do not confuse self-esteem with conceit. This seems to be such a difficult point for most people to grasp. Izett de Forest writes:

> This does not mean yielding to egoism, self-centeredness, "narcissism." Such self-absorption is a severe distortion of character and results from the deep wounding or loss of self respect. It represents a perverted attempt at self-healing, by demanding for one's self, by any and all means, all one can get, more than enough, from the environment to compensate for the wound or the loss. This is a thwarting of the growth process, which depends upon giving rather than getting. Rather than self-love, it is an expression of self-hatred. This is in part what Carl Sandburg meant when he pointed sharply to the different kinds of "pride." I believe in pride, knowing well that the deadliest of the seven deadly sins is named pride. I believe in a pride that prays ever for an awareness of that borderline, where, unless watchful of yourself, you cross over into arrogance, into vanity, into mirror gazing, into misuse and violation of the sacred portions of your personality (1954).

We use "pride" to mean self-respect, and we use "pride" to mean conceit. No wonder we are so confused. Many, out of fear of being conceited, go to the other extreme of depreciating self, thinking this is admirable or even "holy." When one falls into that trap, the future is indeed bleak for the person's happiness.

Equally difficult is to properly mix respect for self apart from other's praise but not going to the extreme of negating praise from others. Izett de Forest quoted D. H. Lawrence on this difficult point:

> There must be brotherly love, a wholeness of humanity. But there must also be pure, separate individuality, separate and proud as a lion or a hawk. There must be both. In the duality lies fulfillment. Man must act in concert with man, creatively and happily. This is greatest happiness. But man must also act separately and distinctly, apart from every other man, single and self responsible and proud with unquenchable pride, moving for himself without reference to his neighbor. These two movements are opposite, yet they do not negate each other. We have understanding. And if we understand, then we balance perfectly between the two motions, we are single, isolated individuals, we are a great concordant humanity, both, and then the rose of perfection transcends us, the rose of the world which has never yet blossomed, but which will blossom from us when we begin to understand both sides and live in both directions, freely and without fear, following the inmost desires of our body and spirit, which arrive us out of the unknown (1954).

When I was younger, my reaction to the previous statement would have been, "Nonsense!" But years and experience have shown that strict logic applied to humans and taken to extremes is not logical; it does not work. There is a further connection between respecting self apart from others, yet not negating praise from others. As one reaches this maturity, he is more able to freely, spontaneously respect others. Thus the whole process of meaningful human interaction is facilitated, and everyone is better for it. Conceit destroys the ability to respect others and is replaced by envy quite often.

As with love, so with self-respect—it is the accumulation of small things, especially the nonverbal exchange of information, that is the key to effective enhancement of this need.

Six

Communication:

Verbal and Nonverbal

We communicate to others, and are communicated to, principally by nonverbal communication. Verbal communication is important. You can study verbal communication for fourteen years in America's formal education systems. Unfortunately, nonverbal communication has not found its way into our formal curricula except on rare occasions.

Albert Mehrabian (1968) reports that 93 percent of our communication is nonverbal; 38 percent is vocal (inflections, intonations, etc.), 55 percent is facial (body posture, etc.), and the remaining 7 percent verbal. Charles Galloway (1968) reports approximately the same percentages. While one may question the high percentages, it is obvious that nonverbal communication needs to be learned, research needs to be done, and application must be made for all people, especially those who are in helping relationships with other humans.

If someone calls you "honey" in a ridiculing tone of voice, the nonverbal communication is what is believed. If someone agrees with you but has what you perceive to be a "smirk" on his face, you interpret the exchange as something less than sincere agreement. Nonverbal communication is inexact; yet it is vitally important in communicating.

Synonyms for, or which include, nonverbal communication are: co-mingling, intrusion, haptics, kinesics, tactile stimulation, body language, etc. A general definition of nonverbal communication is: "Meaning conveyed or communicated without words (written or spoken) or with or in addition to words (written or spoken)."

With children, the socialization process (enculturation) involving verbal and nonverbal communication is often distressful, or may be humorous, particularly if the children are not your own. For example: A couple is visiting my wife and me. Our seven-year-old son is playing on the floor. It is getting late, and I am getting tired. I nonverbally communicate to the couple that it is time to go home. I may stifle a yawn, sneak a look at my watch, stretch my legs, wiggle my feet, let my eyelids droop, or do any of a hundred other things. My son, not having learned "proper" nonverbal communication, may in his innocence blurt out, "Why don't you go home?" Immediately, I half-heartedly laugh and say something like, "Ha, ha, don't pay any attention to him; it is so good to have you over." All the time, I am giving the boy a dirty look. The couple, being enculturated, will smooth it over and probably leave within ten to fifteen minutes (it is hoped!). When they leave, I go back to my son and say, "Don't you ever say anything like that to our friends again." He may respond, "Why, Dad? It was the truth." Then I will give him that profound adult answer, "Because!"

Sooner or later children will learn (we hope)

just what our culture permits us to communicate nonverbally and retain friends, and what it permits us to say verbally—how to communicate, and still continue to have friends.

Another point of vital importance is that most of the things we learn that result in success or failure, in giving and receiving love-belongingness or self-respect, are *learned nonverbally*. For instance, the morning after the episode with the couple, I say to my son, "Take the garbage out." He doesn't want to take the garbage out, so he doesn't look at me. I reach over, grab his chin, look him in the eyes, and repeat my statement. From this example, it is possible that he might learn to look people in the eyes when they talk to him; yet no words have been spoken to that effect. How many people there are who have not learned that and wonder why they have no friends! They may tell a therapist how much they want friends, never realizing why they have none.

Carl Rogers (1964) gave as a possible cause of mental illness: consistent contradictions in a person's verbal and nonverbal communication. Confusion is inevitable, and fear-anxiety has to be the result in the life of such a person. I recommend the book, *A Mingled Yarn*, by Beulah Parker, which illustrates the foregoing points in the life of three siblings. Many of our needs as humans are fulfilled by other humans communicating to us verbally and nonverbally in a consistent, sincere manner.

Be sure to understand that nonverbal communication includes the absence of behavior or overt behavior. For example, a husband reaches over to touch his wife and gets no response at all, but something is communicated. It may be disinterest, hate, getting even, or other feelings, depending upon the circumstances. A father is reading his paper. The daughter comes in and says, "Daddy, I have a pair of new shoes." He barely looks, but says, "They are pretty." Again, something is communicated, but it is not desirable. A little boy, fascinated by a rock, rushes in to his mother, who is washing dishes, and says, "Look what I found." The mother doesn't even respond. What is communicated to the husband, the daughter, the little boy? A message is given and received although there may be no words or actions, or the words and actions may be incongruous.

It is never an isolated "once-in-a-great-while" event, but it is the accumulation of numerous small events which include nonverbal communication that results in a child's feeling secure, loved, respected, and cared for, or the opposite; or in the child's not being sure what the truth is.

There is the case of a teenage girl who is convinced her mother doesn't love her because the mother has a past history of nonverbal communications that convey the lack of love. I, in trying to help them begin a new relationship, mentioned to the mother that she might buy a collar for her daughter's beloved cat on her way home. Her response was typical of her attitude: "Why? What good would that do? I'm here to get help for my daughter!" She had failed to realize that if you don't show interest and love for what your children are interested in and love, you convey a lack of love for the children.

Many times, probably most of the time, humans are not able to verbalize their perceptions of self as confused, worthless, unloved, fearful, bitter, etc. However, they are quite adept at perceiving the same emotion in others, or they are adept at perceiving a desired characteristic in other humans who are successful in that particular area of life.

I am convinced that "having a wonderful personality" means that a person has learned, probably from a model of a significant other or others, how to communicate effectively (both verbally and nonverbally): the successful fulfillment of physical needs, security needs, love-belongingness needs, information needs, etc. Such a person also effectively communicates love and respect to others.

Now, let us turn to some specifics of nonverbal communication, for instance: whether you look into a person's eyes or refuse to, how long you maintain eye contact and the resulting meaning, and how deeply you look into a person's eyes. We all have experienced the following in ourselves or others: sad eyes, eyes that gleam, dry eyes, soft eyes, hard eyes, glares, winks, challenging eyes, red eyes, piercing eyes.

While I was in graduate school, I learned of a riot that was caused by the following incident. A white teacher was talking to a black boy who had been enculturated by the old Negro attitudes. He would not look into the eyes of a white person because that meant disrespect. The white teacher insisted that he respect her by looking at her when she talked to him. Think of the confusion and anxiety that would arise from such a situation!

Next, consider the meaning of a tightly closed mouth, open mouth, gritting teeth, lips stretched tight, tongue sticking out, chewing one's lip, quivering lips, moist lips, dry lips. Depending upon the context, the communication may range from apathy to nervousness to shyness to hate, etc.

The gestures we make with our hands while talking have meaning: closing our fist, having our hands with palms up or down or away from or toward the body, pointing with a finger, folding arms across the chest, and so on.

Our body position is important: leaning toward or away from another human, cocking the head, standing with hands on hips, holding the body rigid or in a relaxed position, sitting or standing, etc.

Human touch is so important in nonverbal communication. Vidal Clay wrote concerning touch and infant care: "It is biologically essential to an infant; it restores the mind and body under stress; and it is the main area by which our need for intimacy is satisfied" (Lobsenz, 1970). I recommend Ashley Montagu's book, *Touching*, for further elaboration on this point.

Next, consider "countenance" and its nonverbal communication. Perhaps the Bible is the best source for illustrations of this: "The king's countenance was changed" (Daniel 5:6); "woman of fair countenance" (2 Samuel 14:27); "his countenance fell" (Genesis 4:5); "A merry heart maketh a cheerful countenance" (Proverbs 15:13). Even our feet speak, according to the Bible: "He speaketh with his feet" (Proverbs 6:13).

Other concepts and specifics for further study in communicating nonverbally are looks, handshakes, mistakes in talking, immediacy or directness in talking, changes in skin color, time spent with individuals, sharing emotions (such as crying) with others, changes in facial expression, how we use our time, feedback, and so forth.

There is a scientific basis for the old adage that actions speak louder than words. Certainly we must recognize and understand nonverbal communication if we are to be effective in our efforts to help other human beings.

Seven

Verbal Communication That Humanizes Relationships

Carl Rogers and F. J. Roethlisberger wrote:

The whole task of psychotherapy is the task of dealing with a failure in communication. The emotionally maladjusted person, the neurotic is in difficulty, first, because communication within himself has broken down and, secondly, because as a result of this his communication with others has been damaged (1952).

I would add the following: The whole task of psychotherapy is the task of dealing with a failure in communication. The emotionally maladjusted person, the neurotic is in difficulty; first, because communication with others has broken down and, second, because as a result of this, communication within himself has been damaged. In other words, it can be either way.

What do we mean by communication within one's self? We mean we are born with needs that demand fulfillment. Yet sometimes we refuse to admit to ourselves that these needs are real, and we may deny the existence of any one or more of these needs.

Communication within is accepting freely in the mind that these needs are real, but communication to others and from others can interfere with the internal communication. This can cause a person literally to fight, tremble, or flee. Perhaps he will turn to substitute ways of fighting, employing the defense mechanisms of attention getting, projection, rationalization, identification, compensation, sublimation, etc. On the other hand, he may choose substitute ways of fleeing, such as the defense mechanisms of negativism, isolation, repression, regression, or fantasy. Or he may choose (unconsciously, of course) psycho-physiological illnesses. Conversion neurosis is another possibility. But the point is this: Communication is the problem within us and between us. For normal people it has not reached the crescendo it has for the neurotic or psychotic, but it is the same problem—only of lesser degree.

Communication consists of two parts: verbal and nonverbal. A. Mehrabian (1968) and Charles Galloway (1968) report that 93 to 94 percent of all communication is nonverbal. That is a very high percentage; yet it seems to be true that if my wife calls me "honey" in a certain tone of voice, the nonverbal wins out. That is 100 percent. Do not err in thinking that lack of behavior is not communicating. Again, if when I enter the house, my wife is reading a newspaper which is in front of her face, and I speak, but there is not a reply, no eye contact: that is communication.

Another important aspect of communication is that there must be general agreement between our verbal and nonverbal communication (Parker, 1972). If in our relations with our children, day in and day out, the verbal and nonverbal communication contradict each other, we can expect our children to be disoriented, confused, and possibly to become either law breakers or mentally ill.

But this is all introductory to the major point, which is verbal communication. Talking is talking. Right? Wrong!

Research has shown three levels of talk (Foley and Bonney, 1966). The first level consists of talk about *things, ideas,* or *events.* All verbal communication must begin here. With most people with whom we converse, it ends here; but if it has never proceeded beyond this with anyone in our whole life, we are lonely and unsure of life and encounter all the many difficulties that loneliness entails.

The second level is a little deeper. It includes talk about nonsignificant groups of people, nonsignificant individuals, significant groups of people—your reference group, and significant others in your life. Yet again, if communication never proceeds beyond this, something is lacking and you feel it; you know it.

The third level of talk is communication with at least one meaningful person in your life about self —your feelings; your emotions, both positive and negative, good feelings, bad feelings; joys and disappointments, love and hate; successes and failures; achieved goals and broken dreams; good things and sinful things.

Think. To whom do you feel closest? Is it not to someone with whom you have communicated at this third level of talk? I am sure it is. Many people are lonely and unsure because they never have had this experience. S. Jourard wrote:

> A choice that confronts every one of us at every moment is this: shall we permit our fellow men to know us as we now are, or shall we seek instead to remain an enigma, an un-

certain quantity, wishing to be seen as something we are not? When we are not truly known by other people in our lives, we are misunderstood. When we are not known, even by family and friends, we join the all too numerous "lonely crowd."

Worse, when we succeed too well in hiding our being from others, we tend to lose touch with our real selves, and this loss of self contributes to illness in its many forms.

Man's life begins to lose its meaning most rapidly when he becomes estranged from his fellows, when they become strangers to him and when he lets himself become a stranger to them. "The key to the self—the soul—is self disclosure" (Jourard, 1964).

I would add *tactful* self-disclosure, not to everyone, but to at least one person, hopefully to two or three.

We are taught from birth, and we teach our children not to talk to others about personal problems. That is all right *unless* we take it to the extreme (as most do) of not talking to parents, or children, or friends, or husband, or wife. The result: We don't even know our parents; we don't really know our children. Husbands and wives can share the same bed and still be strangers after twenty years of marriage.

This is the key I want to give you: *"tactful self-disclosure."* It is the key to deep personal relationships for which we long.

Begin with your loved ones to slowly, tactfully reveal yourself. Be patient; have courage. It will scare you; it will scare them. It is too new. Tactfully teach by words and example that within this home we do it. I will do it. I am not afraid to say I goofed, I was wrong, when that is the way it is. When it is reciprocated, don't panic. Don't be a blamer or a shamer or a convicter. Instead, walk *with* them. You will experience love as never before.

Paul Tournier experienced this and wrote:

It is a question of ceasing to fear one another. Because he fears his pupils, the teacher deals severely with them. It is because the foreman fears his workers—that is, he fears being shown to know less than they on a given point—that he cuts off every discussion with them and finds refuge in silence. For fear of his wife's criticism, a husband will hide the little gift he has bought himself and which he has secretly coveted for a long time.

Tournier continues:

That which helps the patient the most is to discover that he "is not so far off from us as he thinks he is. . . . Stretch out our hand to him. . . . Let us not be afraid of admitting to him our own failings, our inborn flaws; let us draw closer to him." What isolates the patient the most of his life—whether schoolboy, housewife, or worker—is the very thing that isolates us the most: our secrets . . . remorse for our wrongdoings, fears that haunt us, disgust with ourselves that we continually succumb to a certain recurring temptation, inner doubts so vividly in contrast with our air of self confidence, our jealousy and our anger, and even the naive daydreams of glory by which we console ourselves. . . .

No one finds it easy to overcome the inner resistance that obstructs the way to a sincere and deep unveiling of himself.

People come to me, thinking they've found a man who finds interpersonal relationships relatively easy. They can hardly believe me when I tell them it's just the opposite. As a child I was terribly withdrawn. Orphaned quite young, I withdrew into my own lonely little world. . . . Later on as a doctor, I still remained aloof, impersonal, inscrutable. My profession was obstructing my vocation, bringing me deep disappointment . . . a friend challenged me . . . the first step that came clearly to my mind was to unburden myself completely to my wife of many thoughts, memories, fears, and failures which I had never mentioned to her. Such a step seemed impossible to me. I felt I would lose her confidence. . . . It is one thing to speak on the level of ideas, and it is an altogether different thing to speak of one's own soul. When I took this step, my wife answered me, "Now I can be of some help to you!" And she opened up to me in return. We had found the meaning of fellowship (Tournier, 1962).

Some therapists call it ventilation. Freudians call it catharsis. In the Scriptures it is called confession. "Confess your faults one to another, and pray one for another, that you may be healed" (James 5:16).

Yes, it heals. It heals the mind—sometimes even the body. It heals the soul. Tactful self-disclosure is the key to communicating, communicating at the third level, communicating self, communicating meaning, and communicating love.

Eight

Conscience

An understanding of the conscience is absolutely necessary for happiness or good mental health. The conscience is defined as "the process of thought which distinguishes good from bad and which praises the good and condemns the bad" (Vine, 1966).

Other definitions are: "1. the moral, self-critical part of one's self wherein have developed and reside standards of behavior and performance and value judgments, 2. the conscious superego" (Hinsie and Campbell, 1970).

All therapists, sooner or later, have to deal with the hurt conscience of patients.

Two men, Sigmund Freud and O. H. Mowrer, are as far apart in theoretical positions as is possible. The conscience is at the heart of the problem.

In essence, Freud's theory holds that anxiety comes from evil wishes, from acts which the individual would commit if he dared. The alternative view (Mowrer) proposed is that anxiety comes, not from acts which the individual would commit but does not, but from acts which he has committed but wishes he had not" (Mowrer, 1950).

Later on, Mowrer expanded this to include acts the person should have committed but did not (Mowrer, 1969). In other words, commission of acts or omission of acts can cause a troubled conscience—guilt.

There are degrees of a troubled conscience. Pictured on a continuum line, it would be like this:

Figure 7
Degrees of Mental Illness

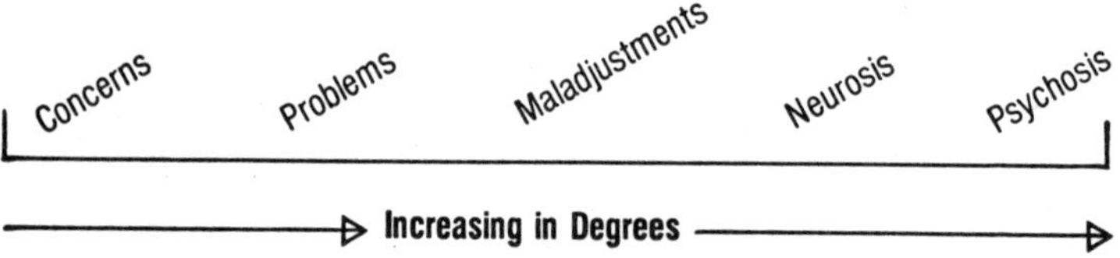

Hinsie and Campbell (1970) wrote, ". . . the function of conscience is to warn the ego to avoid the pain of intense guilt feeling." Conscience is common to all men in all cultures. Accumulated evidence indicates that no primitive people is without conception of right and duty (Walters, 1974).

Concerning guilt, Freedman, Kaplan, and Sadock (1972) write:

It begins developmentally with parental disapproval and becomes internalized as conscience in the course of superego formation. Guilt has normal psychological and social functions, but special intensity or absence of guilt characterizes many mental disorders, such as, depression and antisocial personality respectively.

A few minutes of thought will reveal the impossibility of separating conscience from values. Consider the following needs: (1) physical—food, air, water, sex, etc.; (2) safety; (3) love-belongingness; (4) self-respect; (5) information; (6) understanding; (7) beauty; and (8) self-actualization. How will one satisfy his need for food? Steal? Work? Welfare? Consider different values in respect to each. Consider guilt or lack of guilt. Apply the same reasoning to sex—marital, premarital, extramarital, homosexual, and so on.

Here is a practical outline for mental health: To behave in such a way that all needs can be fulfilled so that there are no guilt feelings.

Here is a practical way to judge different value systems: Do they provide a way or ways to fulfill each need without guilt?

As parents or parent substitutes, do we communicate—verbally and nonverbally—a value system that meets the above criteria?

Fulfilling sexual needs has given humans a great deal of guilt. I have attempted to place this on a continuum line to illustrate too strict a conscience, an

Figure 8
Sexual Fulfillment and Extremes

Any thought or mention of sex is wrong	Fulfilled in marriage	Fulfilled by rape

unquestionable way to fulfill sex, and a pathological way to fulfill sex.

On the left is a value system that some people hold, but which most would agree is a false value system; that is, "If I think of sex, I am awful, a sinner, no good." On the right is a pathological view, "I rape to fulfill my need, and my conscience doesn't bother me at all because I enjoy it and if it feels good, do it." In the center is an unquestionable view, "I fulfill my sex needs with my marriage partner." Certainly, this is an oversimplification; yet, all can agree with it.

We must deal with values. Values determine the feeling of guilt or feeling of guiltless pleasure and its effect on others.

At one time, it was postulated that helpers of people could leave out values. Most would agree with the following view:

> Every Therapist utilizes some concept of man. "One cannot engage in psychotherapy without giving operational evidence of an underlying value orientation and view of human nature." The Therapist's life philosophy, whether it has ever been formally articulated or not, will determine his understanding of man (Walters, 1974).

A Brief Summary and Conclusion

In the preceding chapters, an attempt has been made to introduce eight broad concepts:

1. the concept of order
2. fear-anxiety
3. the needs of humans
4. love
5. self-esteem
6. communication—nonverbal
7. communication—verbal
8. conscience

The more one understands concerning each concept and then forms consistent patterns of behavior based on that understanding, the more daily living is enriched.

The eight areas are interrelated to such an extent that it is impossible to study only one in isolation. Misunderstanding, or ignorance, or misbehavior in one area will bring detrimental consequences not only to that area of one's life but to other areas as well. To varying degrees every area is dependent on every other area.

It is necessary to have a basic understanding of the order of the nine needs within us, each of which is dependent in differing degrees upon other humans for its fulfillment. They are:

1. physical
2. safety-security
3. love-belongingness
4. self-esteem-respect
5. play-laughter-humor
6. information
7. understanding
8. beauty-aesthetic
9. self-actualization

Fulfillment of each of the nine needs is accomplished by the proper reciprocal, verbal and non-verbal, communication. Guilt results if our conscience is violated by the manner in which we fulfill our needs. A good conscience is essential to good mental health. Stress results from unfulfilled needs or a violated conscience. Each need is circular in nature. As soon as a need is fulfilled, we begin to "use it up" and it has to be fulfilled again. Everything written about the interrelationship of the eight broad concepts *equally applies* to the nine basic needs and their interrelationship with each other.

Beyond this, one must realize the "gestalt" of the matter. "Gestalt" means the whole or total is more than the sum of the parts. The total human is more than the sum of the eight categories plus the nine needs. When one sees a movie, one does not see separate frames, each different from every other frame. If the projector is stopped, individual frames can be examined, but one would not be viewing a movie. So it is when we study humans and study each need and category of human behavior.

A rejection in our mind of any of these principles will not change the situation except to lead to consequences of some type of unhappiness. A degree of dependency on others, while avoiding the extreme positions, must also be accepted for the reality that exists. An engine cannot reject oil and operate smoothly or efficiently.

Discovering ourselves in order to also understand others is complex, but not impossible.

Index

Names and Subjects

Index of Figures

References

Allen, R. D. Guidance and counseling. *Review of Educational Research*, 1933, *3*, 214-221.

Allport, G. W. A psychological approach to the study of love and hate. In P. A. Sorokin, *Explorations in Altruistic Love and Behavior*. Boston: The Beacon Press, 1950.

Ansbacher, H. L. *Adlerian Psychology: A Basic Theory*. (Tape recording.) New York: McGraw-Hill, Inc., 1969.

Barclay, W. *New Testament Words*. Philadelphia: The Westminster Press, 1974.

Bleibtreu, J. N. *The Parable of the Beast*. New York: The Macmillan Co., 1968.

Campbell, A. *The Sense of Well-being in America*. New York: McGraw Hill Book Co., 1981.

Cooley, C. H. *Human Nature and the Social Order*. Boston: Scribner, 1902.

Coopersmith, S. *Studies in Self Esteem*. Scientific American. February 1968.

Coopersmith S. *The Antecedents of Self Esteem*. San Francisco: W. H. Freeman, 1967.

De Forest, I. *The Leaven of Love.* New York: Harper & Brothers, 1954.

Dimsdale, J. E., & Moss, J. "Plasma Catecholamines in Stress and Exercise." *Journal of American Medical Association,* 1980, 243, No. 4, 340-342.

"Doctor Will Offer First Evidence People Can be Scared to Death." *Charlotte Observer,* February 24, 1980.

Dusky, L. "Who Is My Daughter?" *Newsweek,* October 15, 1980.

Eiger, M. D., & Olds, S. W. *The Complete Book of Breastfeeding.* New York: Workman Publishing Co., Inc., 1972.

Fanshel, D., & Shinn, E. B. *Children in Foster Care.* New York: Columbia University Press, 1978.

Flanagan, J. C. "A Research Approach to Improving Our Quality of Life." *American Psychologist,* February, 1978.

Foley, W. J., & Bonney, W. C. "A Developmental Model for Counseling Groups." *Personnel and Guidance Journal,* February, 1966, pp. 576-580.

Freedman, A. M., Kaplan, H. I. & Sadock, B. J. *Modern Synopsis of Comprehensive Textbook of Psychiatry.* Baltimore: Williams & Wilkins, 1972.

Fromm-Reichmann, F. *Principles of Intensive Psychotherapy.* Chicago: The University of Chicago Press, 1967.

Galloway, C. "Nonverbal Communication." *The Instructor,* April 1968.

Glasser, W. *Reality Therapy.* New York: Harper & Row, 1965.

Hinsie, L. E., & Campbell, R. J. *Psychiatric Dictionary.* New York: Oxford Press, 1970.

Hite, S. *The Hite Report.* New York: Macmillan Publishing Co., Inc., 1976.

Holmes, T. H., & Rahe, R. H. "Social Readjustment Rating Scale." *Journal of Psychosomatic Research,* 1967, 11, 213-218.

Hudson, P. "Mysterious Disease Kills Children." *Asheville Citizen,* January 23, 1971.

Jourard, S. M. *The Transparent Self.* New York: D. Van Nostrand Co., 1964.

Katchadavian, H. A., & Lunde, D. T. *Fundamentals of Human Sexuality.* New York: Holt, Rinehart and Winston Inc., 1972.

Kauffman, J. F. "The Individual and the Search for Self Esteem." *Journal of National Association Women Deans and Counselors,* Fall, 1968.

Kittel, G., ed. *Theological Dictionary of the New Testament* (ten volumes). Grand Rapids, Michigan: Wm. B. Eerdmans Publishing Company, 1964.

Lewis, C. S. *The Four Loves.* New York: Harcourt Brace Jovanovich, Inc., 1960.

Lobsenz, Norman M. "The Loving Message in a Touch." *Woman's Day.* February, 1970.

London, P. *The Modes and Morals of Psychotherapy.* New York: Holt, Rinehart, & Winston, 1964.

Maslow, A. H. *Motivation and Personality* (second ed.). New York: Harper & Row Publishers, Inc., 1970.

May, R. *Love and Will.* New York: Dell Publishing Co., Inc., 1969.

Mayor, W. E. *Code of Conduct.* (tape recording.) 1956.

Mehrabian, A. "Communication without Words." *Psychology Today.* September, 1968.

Menninger, K. *Love against Hate.* New York: Harcourt Brace & World, Inc., 1942.

Money, J. "Sex Hormones and Other Variables in Human Eroticism." In W. C. Young (ed.) *Sex and Internal Secretions* (2 vol.) (chapter 22), Baltimore: Williams and Wilkins, Co., 1961.

Montagu, A. *Touching.* New York: Columbia University Press, 1971.

Mowrer, O. H. *A Re-evaluation of Psychoanalysis.* (tape recording.) New York: McGraw Hill Book Co., 1969.

Munn, N. L. *Introduction to Psychology.* Boston: Houghton-Mifflin Co., 1962.

Neiger, S. "Overcoming Sexual Inadequacy. (cassette tape, no. 4.) *Important New Findings on Human Sexual Response.* Chicago, Ill.: Human Development Institute, 1973.

Osol, A., ed. *Gould Medical Dictionary* (third ed.). New York: McGraw Hill Book Co., 1972.

Parker, B. *A Mingled Yarn.* New York: Yale University Press, 1972.

Pavlov, I. P. *Conditioned Reflexes.* (Translated and edited by G. V. Annp.) New York: Dover Publications, Inc., 1960.

Poovey, C. "Adoptive Search Goes On." *Winston Salem Journal,* October 21, 1980.

Ratcliff, J. D. "New Search for the Fountain of Youth." *Reader's Digest,* December, 1963, pp. 69-75.

Rigdon, R. M. "Concepts in Helping Other Human Beings—Part 1": *Tennessee Public Welfare Record,* 37, 1, 1974.

Rigdon, R. M. "Concepts in Helping Other Human Beings—Part 2: Communications." *Tennessee Public*

Welfare Record, 37, 2, 1974.

Rigdon, R. M. "Concepts in Helping Other Human Beings—Part 3: Homeostasis and Self-respect." *Tennessee Public Welfare Record,* 37, 3, 1974.

Rigdon, R. M. "Concepts in Helping Other Human Beings—Part 4: The Human Conscience." *Tennessee Public Welfare Record,* 37, 4, 1974.

Rigdon, R. M. "The Differentiation of the Need for Sex, Temptation, and Lust." *Restoration Quarterly,* 21, 4, 1978.

Rigdon, R. M. "The Need of Self Respect and How It Differs from Pride or Conceit." *Restoration Quarterly,* 20, 1, 1977.

Rogers, C. R., & Roethlisberger, F. J. "Barriers and Gateways to Communication." *Harvard Business Review,* July-August, 1952.

Selye, H. *The Stress of Life.* New York: McGraw Hill Book Co., 1956.

Sheehy, G. *Passages.* New York: Bantam Books, Inc., 1974.

Slusher, H. S. *Man, Sport and Existence.* Philadelphia: Lea & Fibiger, 1967.

Stone, A., & Sonte, H. *Marriage Manual* (Rev. & Ed.). New York: Simon and Schuster, Inc., 1968.

Taylor, K. T. *Love as Mystery, Experience, and Creative Power.* (tape recording #AT372.) Berkeley, California: 1977.

Thayer, J. H. (Translator). *Greek-English Lexicon of the New Testament.* Grand Rapids, Michigan: Zondervan Publishing House, 1967.

Thurman, H. (Title unknown.) An Address Delivered at Boston University, May 4, 1968.

Toffler, A. *Future Shock.* New York: Bantam Books, 1971.

Tournier, P. *Escape from Loneliness.* Philadelphia: The Westminster Press, 1962.

Trainer, J. *Physiologic Foundations for Marriage Counseling.* St. Louis, Mo.: C. V. Mosby Co., 1965.

Vaillant, G. E. *Adaptation to Life.* Boston: Little, Brown & Co., 1977.

Vine, W. E. *Expository Dictionary of New Testament Words.* Old Tappan, New Jersey: Fleming H. Revell Co., 1966.

Walters, O. S. *The Anatomy of Psychotherapy.* (Unpublished mimeographed article), 1974.

Williams, D. D. *The Spirit and the Forms of Love.* New York: Harper and Row Publishers, 1968.